Fort Anderson:

Battle for Wilmington

by

Chris E. Fonvielle, Jr.

Savas Publishing Company

Manufactured in the United States of America

Fort Anderson: Battle for Wilmington
by Chris E. Fonvielle, Jr.

©1999 by Chris E. Fonvielle, Jr.
Maps © by Mark A. Moore
Cover illustration by Chuck Leise

Includes bibliographical references and index

Savas Publishing Company
202 First Street, SE, Suite 103A
Mason City, Iowa 50401   1-800-732-3669

Printing Number
10 9 8 7 6 5 4 3 2 1

ISBN 1-882810-40-6
First hardcover edition

ISBN 1-882810-24-4
First softcover edition

This book is printed on 60-lb., acid-free stock. The paper in this book meets or exceeds the guidelines for permanence and durability of the Committee on Production Guidelines for Book Longevity of the Council on Library Resources.

*To my wife Nancy
and our daughters,
Mary Katherine and Anne Fletcher,
for their love, encouragement and understanding.*

Table of Contents

Maps

My introduction to Fort Anderson, Brunswick Town State Historic Site, and the Lower Cape Fear region came in mid-December 1963. At that time "Operation *Cairo*, Inc." was underway on Mississippi's Yazoo River. As a National Park Service historian stationed at the Vicksburg National Military Park, I had long been associated with the *Cairo* project that had then entered a critical stage with the recovery and cataloging of thousands of artifacts from the sunken Union ironclad. One of my supervisors was Jean C. "Pinky" Harrington, a pioneer in historical archaeology and Chief of Interpretation for the Service's Southeast Region. Pinky sent me, along with two of his staff members, to Wilmington, North Carolina, to meet with archaeologist Stanley South and his associates. We were to review with them onsite the challenges they had encountered in recovering and preserving objects and cargo from the sunken Civil War blockade runner *Modern Greece*.

South, then project archaeologist, had his office at Brunswick Town. Apprised of my interest in the Civil War, its fortifications and material culture, South called my attention to Fort Anderson. My unfamiliarity with either the fort or its context was compounded by the limited removal of dense vegetation that had hidden the earthworks for years prior to South's efforts. As a result, I failed to appreciate the fortifications' scale and the state of their preservation.

I next saw Fort Anderson in the first week of October 1993. The occasion was the 24th Annual Congress of Civil War Round Table Associates held in Wilmington. Three months before, the city on the Cape Fear had hosted the final public meeting of the Civil War Sites Advisory Commission, a study group established by the United States Congress. Because of a crowded schedule and limited time, the Commissioners--although they traveled to Bentonville, New Bern and Fort Fisher--were unable to go to Fort Anderson.

With no public meeting and more time, Chairman Jerry Russell scheduled a Fort Anderson field trip for the Round Table Associates. As in every Associates' Congress since its first meeting in 1976 that highlighted Antietam, I led the battlefield walks. This had the potential for some embarrassment because of my unfamiliarity with Fort Anderson and Brunswick Town. Fate intervened in the person of Chris E. Fonvielle, Jr. Wilmington born and reared, and with graduate degrees from East Carolina University and the University of South Carolina, Fonvielle is a walking encyclopedia of information on the military and cultural history of the Lower Cape Fear. Equally important, he had walked these sites and knew the landscape. Better yet, he shared with me chapters of his manuscript focusing on Fort Anderson. Thanks to Chris' scholarship and generosity, I completed a crash course on Fort Anderson, its context and environment in time to lead the field trip to the site. None of the Associates were the wiser. Participants in the field trip were as impressed as I with the magnificent condition and scale of the earthworks. They likewise found the ruins of Brunswick Town romantic, and the visitor center and its exhibits equal to the high standards associated with the North Carolina State Historic Sites.

Having sensed the value of the chapters of Fonvielle's Wilmington Campaign study which had bailed me out in 1993, I was delighted with the manuscript's publication by Savas Publishing Company in 1997 under the title *The Wilmington Campaign: Last Rays of Departing Hope.* Now, to enhance what was a blockbuster, Fonvielle has gone to the well again. This time he narrowed the focus by enriching and broadening the story of Fort Anderson to include its 18th century antecedent, Brunswick Town and its halcyon days, and concludes with its mid-20th century rediscovery and the preservation and interpretation of the most magnificent Civil War eastern coastal fortification I have walked. Thank you, Chris Fonvielle, for intro-

ducing us to Fort Anderson, and the gallant men in butternut and blue who stood tall and were counted in that great struggle of 134 years ago that gave a new dimension to our nation.

Edwin C. Bearss
Historian Emeritus
National Park Service

Fort Anderson has been in my blood for as long as I can remember. As a boy growing up in the 1950s and 1960s, I visited the old Confederate fort at the Brunswick Town State Historic Site near Wilmington, North Carolina, with my parents, siblings and classmates on field trips, picnics and outings. My mother, in particular, took an interest in the historic place. As the hostess of her own TV talk show, 1963-1971, she occasionally interviewed Dr. Stanley A. South, the Brunswick Town-Fort Anderson project archaeologist, for broadcast on WWAY TV-3, the local ABC affiliate. I enthusiastically accompanied her excursions to the area to observe Dr. South's ongoing excavations and marvel at the colonial and Civil War artifacts he and his crew pulled from the earth.

Bitten by the archaeology bug myself, I kept my eyes glued to the ground in hopes of finding a dropped minie ball, a military uniform button or an iron cannonball fragment as I traipsed about the Civil War fort, which was built on top of the colonial ghost town of Brunswick. My diligent search never bore fruit, so imagine my consternation when my then six-year-old brother John, who was younger than I and not especially interested in history, found an iron grape shot along the marshy shoreline of the Cape Fear River at Fort Anderson. Somehow the artifact ended up in my possession, though it will always really be John's.

The Brunswick Town-Fort Anderson State Historic Site is my favorite spot in the Lower Cape Fear. Beautiful, serene, alluring, mysterious and romantic are adjectives that come to mind when attempting to describe the area. I have never seen a ghost at the site, but the life force there is undeniably strong. As you walk about the property, it is easy to visualize the hustle and bustle of the colonial seaport or hear the reports of Confederate cannon fire inside Fort Anderson.

My desire to learn about Fort Anderson began all those years ago when I first roamed the site. It deepened when I served as the last curator of the Blockade Runners of the Confederacy Museum at Carolina Beach, North Carolina, 1979-1983. Subsequently, I devoted some of my graduate work at East Carolina University and the University of South Carolina to the Fort Anderson story, which historians had overlooked. Those efforts led to "Outflanked," a chapter on the 1865 Battle of Fort Anderson in my first book, *The Wilmington Campaign: Last Rays of Departing Hope* (Savas Publishing, 1997).

The current Brunswick Town State Historic Site manager, James A. Bartley, urged me to narrow my focus by writing a monograph on the complete history of Fort Anderson, 1862-1865. Fort Anderson, it seems, has been plagued by a reputation as the Cape Fear's "other" Confederate fort, always playing second fiddle to Fort Fisher on the opposite side of the Cape Fear River. Indeed, Fort Fisher was the Confederacy's most powerful seacoast fortification protecting the most popular blockade-running seaport, and the two Fort Fisher battles in late 1864 and early 1865 were the largest U.S. Army-Navy operations of the Civil War.

Fort Anderson was also important to Confederate Wilmington. It was second in size and strength only to Fort Fisher among the forts and batteries guarding the port, and it protected the river and western land approaches to the city. By late January 1865, Lt. Gen. U.S. Grant was so determined to capture the Tarheel town that he came to the Cape Fear to personally plan the attack on Wilmington by way of Fort Anderson. Perhaps just as intriguing about the Fort Anderson story, revealed to me through the letters, diaries, and recollections of the men on both sides who served and fought there, were its connections with President Abraham Lincoln's assassination. The threads of Cape Fear history are sewn far and wide.

And so this project, *Fort Anderson: Battle for Wilmington*, began innocently enough long, long ago. My involvement in the fort's story was implanted, inspired, and nurtured along the way by family, friends, and colleagues alike. First and foremost, I want to thank my publisher, Theodore P. Savas, for showing a passionate interest in my work in Civil War history, and for his willingness to publish this follow-up to *Last Rays*. With his usual excitement, Ted immediately agreed to my suggestion that I delve more deeply into the Fort Anderson story and to publish my findings.

All but one of the maps which grace the pages of Fort Anderson were drawn by Civil War historian and incomparable cartographer Mark A. Moore. With good reason, Mark has been dubbed the "Jedediah Hotchkiss (Stonewall Jackson's map maker) of the twentieth century." One look at Mark's maps confirms the credibility of his sobriquet.

I am again indebted to Edwin C. Bearss for his willingness to review the *Fort Anderson* manuscript (as he kindly did for *Last Rays*), offer suggestions on how it might be improved, and for accepting my invitation to write the Foreword. For many years, Ed served as the chief historian of the U.S. National Park Service. Since his "retirement,"

he has been in high demand for speaking engagements and tours of America's battlefields.

Ed and I first visited Fort Anderson together in October 1993, when he was leading a tour of the Wilmington Campaign for the annual meeting of the Congress of Civil War Round Tables. It was that same weekend that I met Ted Savas, who showed a deep interest in my manuscript on the campaign.

After visiting other Cape Fear Civil War sites, the Round Table Associates were given a grand tour of Fort Anderson by Ed Bearss. Despite the fact that no published work on the fort's history existed, Ed related in impressive detail the 1865 battle there—troop and warship deployment, movements, casualties, human interest vignettes, etc. I had heard that he was a walking encyclopedia of American military history, and his remarkable tour of Fort Anderson that autumn afternoon certainly made a believer out of me.

It appears that Ed, too, has fallen under Fort Anderson's mystical spell, as he has returned to the place twice since that fateful 1993 visit. This past May, I had the honor of assisting him in leading the Chicago Civil War Round Table on a tour of the Wilmington Campaign sites. Obviously, we spent much of our time at Fort Anderson.

A special thanks also goes out to the staff of the Brunswick Town-Fort Anderson State Historic Site, especially James A. Bartley, Tammy Bangert, Greg Bland, Elbert Felton, Ron Gooding and Brenda Marshburn. These ladies and gentlemen always make me feel welcome at the site and always make me laugh. Jimmy Bartley and Bert Felton especially have gone beyond the call of duty to assist me in my research.

I would be remiss not to acknowledge my mother's role in all of this. Though I do not recall the details, I probably first visited Fort Anderson with her. She has always been interested in my passions and pursuits.

Thanks, too, to Annie Gray Sprunt Holt, who graciously invited me into her family's historic home at Orton Plantation. It was my first tour inside the colonial-era dwelling, where the original architect of Fort Anderson lived while he worked on his nearby fortification.

I also acknowledge with appreciation the assistance of Bennett Langley, who read the *Fort Anderson* manuscript and, over the years, has shared with me his vast knowledge of Cape Fear Civil War history.

I would also like to thank the following people who provided me with source material, photographs, leads and/or encouragement during this project: Thomas E. Beaman, Jr., Susan Taylor Block, Mike Budziszewski, Robert Calder, Susie Carson, Diane Cashman, Sarah B. Chapman, Penn Croom, Monalisa DiAngelo, Mike Edge, Joseph E. Elmore, Mark Jacobson, Don Koonce, Don Lennon, Elizabeth Lewis, Pat Marshburn, Steve McAllister, James McCallum, Jim McKee, Dick and Ellen McMann, Lee Merideth, Tom Morgan, Charlotte Murchison, Jerry Netherland, Jonathan Noffke, Jerry Parnell, Jackie Phillippe at Coastal Camera & Photo, Jim Pleasants, Nan Pope and Richard Corcoran at Precision Press, Dave Pruett, William M. Reaves, Dave Roth of *Blue & Gray*, Steven J. Selenfriend, Joseph Sheppard, Anna Sherman, D. "Mule" Skinner, Stanley South, Ben Steelman, Chris Suiter, Jay Taylor, John Douglas Taylor, Walker Taylor III, Beverly Tetterton, John Vause, Mark Weldon, Dickie Wolfe and Steve L. Zerbe.

My appreciation also goes out to Chuck Leise of Wilmington, a professional artist and inquisitive student of world history, who spent many hours with me discussing the Battle of Fort Anderson and studying battle illustrations to produce an accurate depiction of Fort Anderson's Battery B under attack by Union warships. His keen eye for detail and exactness is apparent on the cover art of *Fort Anderson: Battle for Wilmington.*

My wife, Nancy and our two daughters, Mary Katherine and Anne Fletcher, have patiently indulged my many hours exploring Fort Anderson, researching its fascinating story, and tapping away on this keyboard in my office. When I began this study (having just completed *Last Rays*), Mary Katherine observed somewhat facetiously, "I guess we won't see you again for another two years." Rest assured, however, that as important as the history of the old Cape Fear is to me, my girls are my life, and I thank the Good Lord for blessing me with them.

May the charm of Fort Anderson and the story of the men in gray and blue who served and fought there instill you with appreciation, curiosity, and a passion for the past, as they have me.

Chris E. Fonvielle, Jr.
Wilmington, North Carolina
October 12, 1998

Chapter 1

The Defenses

Military engineers constructed a vast network of earthen forts and batteries to protect the Confederacy's most important blockade running seaport at Wilmington, North Carolina. *Author's Collection.*

General Johnson Hagood faced a desperate situation. Dispatches from his cavalry, together with testimony from prisoners and deserters, convinced the South Carolina brigadier that as many as 7,000 Federal troops were encircling his position at Fort Anderson. The Confederate garrison of almost 2,300 men was much too small to oppose the Union flanking force, as well as the blue-clad brigades gathered in front of the fort and the flotilla of enemy warships positioned on the Cape Fear River. Hagood was inclined to evacuate the fort in an effort to save his command, but such a drastic move required the authorization of his superior officer.

With time working against him, Hagood telegraphed Maj. Gen. Robert F. Hoke, headquartered at Sugar Loaf on the opposite side of the river, and expressed concern that his command was on the verge of being surrounded. Hagood cautioned Hoke that if the commanding general ordered the fort abandoned, the

withdrawal would have to be executed at once. The Federals would surely strike at sunrise, and the Confederates controlled only two narrow avenues of escape—the Wilmington Road and the Orton Plantation causeway. Both of these routes would take the retreating soldiers dangerously close to the Union troops advancing on Fort Anderson's right flank.

Hoke sat on the horns of a dilemma. Despite Hagood's dire message, he was reluctant to order the abandonment of the important fort. He recalled his own instructions from the high command that, except in the case of an emergency, Fort Anderson must be held. A retreat from there would not only give the Federals a key stronghold in the Lower Cape Fear, but would also seriously threaten the fall of the second most important city in the Confederacy—Wilmington, North Carolina.[1]

When this engraving appeared in *Gleason's Pictorial Drawing Room Companion* in 1853, Wilmington was North Carolina's largest city and one of the world's largest naval stores markets. View of Wilmington's waterfront looking southeastward from Point Peter, at the confluence of the Cape Fear River and the Northeast Cape Fear River. *Gleason's Pictorial Drawing Room Companion*

Wilmington is a beautiful old city nestled on a sloping sand ridge on the east side of the Cape Fear River, about twenty-six miles from where it empties into the Atlantic Ocean in southeastern North Carolina. Founded in 1732, it is one of the state's oldest communities. For much of its history, Wilmington was also the Tarheel State's largest city. On the eve of the Civil War, Wilmington boasted a population of about 10,000 people, a third of whom were slaves and free blacks. It grew from a small colonial trading post at the point where the Cape Fear River and Northeast Cape Fear River meet, to a bustling seaport with an active mercantile trade, two commercial shipbuilding yards, two iron and copper works, a sword and button factory, five banks, several turpentine distilleries, cotton presses and saw mills and three railroads. In fact, one of the railroads—the Wilmington & Weldon line—was the longest in the world upon completion of its 162-mile stretch to Weldon, North Carolina in 1840. Wilmington did not enjoy the fame or commercial success of Charleston and Savannah, but the city grew steadily and prospered during the antebellum period as North Carolina's most active seaport

and one of the world's largest suppliers of naval stores. During the Civil War, Wilmington emerged as the Confederacy's most important seaport.

By the summer of 1864, only the capital of Richmond was of more value to the Southern cause than Wilmington. For the better part of three years, the Carolina "city by the sea" was the favorite port of call for blockade running ships carrying supplies vital to the South's war effort. Unable to compete with the industrial might of the North, the Confederacy turned to the European market—especially Great Britain—for firearms, artillery, ammunition, sabers, bayonets, lead, iron, wool for uniforms, brass buttons, medicines, blankets, boots, shoes, tools, food, and other such provisions that could not be easily procured at home. To reach the Confederacy, however, blockade runners had to elude U.S. Navy gunboats blockading the South's coast. At 3,549 miles, the lengthy shoreline forced Union blockading vessels to focus their main efforts against the Confederacy's dozen major seaports, including Charleston, Savannah, New Orleans, Mobile, Norfolk, and Wilmington.

Wilmington was ideally situated for blockade running because it was close to the British transshipment points of Bermuda and Nassau in the Bahamas. Transatlantic merchantmen carried supplies earmarked for the Confederacy from Britain to Bermuda and Nassau, where they were transferred to light draft and swift blockade runners for the final dash into Southern seaports. Blockade runners liked Wilmington because it could be accessed by one of two inlets—Old Inlet, the main bar and southern entrance into the Cape Fear River, and New Inlet, a shallow strait five miles to the northeast. Bald Head Island and Frying Pan Shoals separated Old and New Inlets, offering blockade runners a choice of entrance into and exit from the harbor. The dual passageways also made it virtually impossible for Union ships to halt the clandestine maritime trade at the Cape Fear. One Confederate official claimed that as many as 100 different blockade running vessels operated in and out of Wilmington during the war, and more times than not they eluded even the most vigilant Union blockaders. Making it even more difficult for the U.S. Navy, Wilmington itself was located far out of range of naval bombardment.

After the fall of Norfolk, Virginia and the North Carolina sound towns of New Bern and Beaufort in the spring of 1862, Wilmington was the closest open seaport to the Virginia battle-front. Good interior lines of communication, which served as natural pipelines for sending supplies and troops to the front, connected Wilmington with key points south, north and west. The Cape Fear River was navigable all the way to Fayetteville, North Carolina, 100 miles northwest of Wilmington, and three railroads connected Wilmington to other prominent cities in the Carolinas and the Old Dominion. The most important of these rail lines was the Wilmington & Weldon Railroad, which by 1861 had been extended another ninety miles to connect the North Carolina port town with

By the summer of 1864, only the capital of Richmond was of more value to the Southern cause than Wilmington.

Perhaps as many as 100 different blockade runners operated in and out of Wilmington during the war, including the *Let Her Rip* shown here.
Courtesy of Charles V. Peery

Petersburg, Virginia. The Wilmington & Weldon served as General Robert E. Lee's main supply route in the war's last year.

To protect Wilmington and the railroads and the inlets utilized by blockade runners, Confederate engineers built a vast complex of forts, batteries, and fieldworks throughout southeastern North Carolina. Artillery batteries virtually ringed the city, while a series of outer defenses guarded the environs from an overland attack and an enemy invasion along the Atlantic shoreline.

The strongest and best-armed forts in the Lower Cape Fear were built to protect the harbor's inlets for blockade runners. Forts Caswell and Campbell and Battery Shaw on Oak Island, and Fort Holmes on Bald Head Island guarded Old Inlet. Despite Old Inlet's status as the main bar, however, blockade runners preferred using New Inlet. The heavier-draft blockading U.S. gunboats could not ply the inlet's shallow and intricate channel as could the light draft blockade running vessels. The passageway was also well protected.

To safeguard New Inlet, engineers constructed the largest and strongest seacoast fortification in the Confederacy: Fort Fisher. The fort and its auxillary works were located near the end of Federal Point (called Confederate Point by Southerners during the war), a narrow peninsula bounded by the Cape Fear River on the west and the Atlantic Ocean on the east. The sand spit tapered to a point at New Inlet. The immense two-sided earthen fortification comprised a series of elevated gun batteries mounting forty-seven pieces of seacoast artillery, connected by a broad rampart. Fort Fisher's land face stretched 500 yards from the river to the sea, and then southward along the ocean's shoreline for about 1,300 yards. Both Confederate and Union observers deemed Fort Fisher impregnable against a naval attack. Dubbed the Gibraltar of the South, the massive fort was the key to Wilmington's defense.

Supplementing the fortifications protecting Old and New Inlets were defenses constructed along the banks of the Cape Fear River between the passageways and Wilmington to guard the water approaches to the city. Fort Johnston (renamed Fort Pender by the Confederates in 1864) at Smithville, a small village on the west side of the Cape Fear River about two miles from Old Inlet, overlooked the town's harbor and lower estuary. Battery Lamb on Reeves Point five miles north of Smithville (present day Southport) commanded the river behind New Inlet and Fort Fisher. A series of four large earthen batteries along the Cape Fear River's east bank three miles south of Wilmington guarded the approach to the city's docks.[2]

The most notable of all the Lower Cape Fear's interior fortifications was Fort Anderson. Built atop the ruins of Brunswick, a colonial ghost town, Fort Anderson was positioned on low bluffs along the west bank of the Cape Fear River in Brunswick County, roughly halfway between Wilmington and the Atlantic Ocean. Like Fort Fisher, Fort Anderson was an immense earthen fort. Despite the similarity in appearance and strength of the two forts, however, Fort Anderson has always been considered the Lower Cape Fear's "other" Confederate fort. It was overshadowed by Fort Fisher's more strategic location, Fisher's reputation as the South's most powerful seacoast fortification, and, in the end, by the two critical battles fought there in 1864 and 1865—the largest U.S. Army-Navy operations of the war. But Fort Anderson was also important to Confederate Wilmington.

In the days before the American Revolution, Brunswick Town, or "Old Brunswick" as locals call it, was Great Britain's main port of entry in North Carolina. Founded by Maurice and Roger Moore in 1726, Brunswick quickly rose to prominence as the British empire's major supplier of naval stores (tar, pitch and turpentine) as well as board lumber. Brunswick's surrounding forest abounded with long leaf pine and live

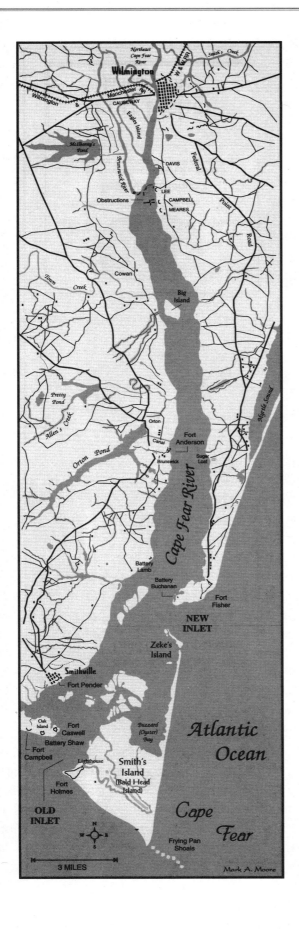

With the exception of Charleston, Wilmington, North Carolina was the most heavily defended Confederate city on the Atlantic seaboard during the Civil War. Engineers constructed a vast network of forts and batteries to protect the Confederacy's major blockade running seaport, which was located twenty-six miles up the Cape Fear River. As long as Southern forces controlled the Cape Fear River, blockade running ships could bring in supplies vital to the Confederacy's war effort. The most powerful and best armed forts in the region were erected at the harbor's two entrances utilized by blockade runners: Old Inlet to the south and New Inlet five miles to the northwest. Fortifications were also built at strategic points along the Cape Fear River to protect the land approaches to Wilmington, as well as the city's railroads. Fort Anderson was built along the river's west bank at Brunswick Point, fifteen miles below the city, to cover the river channel and the main road leading from the town of Smithville near Old Inlet to Wilmington. Fort Anderson would be the target of an overwhelming combined Union attack in February 1865.

Artist Don Mayhew's rendition of Brunswick Town's Public House and Tailor Shop, built on the Cape Fear riverfront about 1732. The foundation ruins have been excavated and are visible today. *Brunswick Town State Historic Site*

oak trees, the byproducts of which helped maintain the royal navy.

No more than 250 residents and their slaves ever lived in Brunswick Town, yet it was the seat of government and ecclesiastical authority in the colony. Royal Governors Arthur Dobbs and William Tryon both lived there for a time, and it was also the home of St. Philip's Church, one of two grand Anglican houses of worship in the parish. The massive three-foot thick brick walls of St. Philip's still stand like a lone sentinel watching guard over the desolate Brunswick site. Governor Dobbs is buried within the edifice, and in the adjacent churchyard repose a number of renowned citizens, including Benjamin Smith, an aide-de-camp to Gen. George Washington and post-Revolutionary War governor of North Carolina; Alfred Moore, speaker of the North Carolina House of Commons and a justice of the U.S. Supreme Court; and William Dry, collector of customs at Brunswick and one of the Lower Cape Fear's more famous patriots.

For a time, Brunswick endured economic woes, storms, and war to survive. One of the most serious threats to the town came from Spanish privateers. Determined to protect the remnants of her once powerful New World empire, Spain challenged the expanding English presence along the Atlantic seaboard. In early September 1748, two Spanish sloops ascended the Cape Fear River to attack Brunswick Town. The unprotected townspeople were caught woefully off guard by the appearance of the enemy vessels and fled into the countryside. Despite their fear, the Brunswick men soon regrouped and, aided by local militiamen, counterattacked the Spaniards, who were looting and pillaging the town. In the ensuing battle, the Spanish sloop *Fortuna* inexplicably blew up, killing and wounding most of her crew. The survivors beat a hasty retreat from the Cape Fear. Among the items Brunswick's residents salvaged from the derelict enemy vessel was a beautiful oil portrait of Jesus Christ with the crown of thorns, called *Ecce Homo*. The painting, perhaps done by Francisco Pacheco in the early seventeenth century, was given to the congregation of St. James Anglican Church in nearby Wilmington, where it hangs today. Brunswick's vulnerability to attack motivated the English Crown to beef up its defenses of the important colonial port by completing the construction of Fort Johnston near the mouth of the Cape Fear harbor.[3]

Ironically, it was not war with Spain but the emergence of Wilmington upriver that ultimately doomed Brunswick Town. As one observer noted, "Wilmington first became Brunswick's rival and then its gravedigger." Brunswick found it difficult to compete with Wilmington, which was more conveniently located for both commercial and population growth, and more safely tucked away from hurricanes that threatened the Carolina coast during the summer and autumn months. Wilmington received the trade of planters along the upper branches of both the Cape Fear River and Northeast Cape Fear River, as well as more political support, and flourished, resulting in a "general exodus" at Brunswick Town by 1775. The Revolutionary War, for all practical purposes, sealed Brunswick's fate. British troops sacked the town when they raided the Lower Cape Fear in the spring of 1776, and it lost its political leverage when the new state legislature moved Brunswick County's seat of government to Lockwood's Folly, a place of relative safety from the Redcoats.[4]

A few original residents and some squatters lived among the ruins of Old Brunswick after the War for Independence and during the early nineteenth century, but according to one account, "the entire town site was sold for $4.25 in 1842" to Dr. Frederick J. Hill, the owner of adjacent Orton Plantation. When Confederate engineers surveyed the location twenty years later, a veritable jungle of scrub oaks, vines, bushes, and trees had reclaimed Brunswick Town's decayed buildings and the royal governors' palace at Russellborough, a stone's throw north of the vanished town. "Flourishing shrubbery" was even growing on top of the walls of St. Philip's Church.[5]

An entourage of Confederate officers and engineers went ashore at Brunswick on March 22, 1862, one of the first stopping points on a two-day tour of the District of the Cape Fear defenses by the new district commander, Brig. Gen. Samuel Gibbs French. Officially, General French was given command of the district on March 15, succeeding Brig. Gen. Joseph Reid Anderson, who was temporarily promoted to head the Department of North Carolina. French arrived at his new headquarters in Wilmington on March 22 and immediately embarked upon an inspection trip of his domain.[6]

Brunswick struck French as an ideal site to build a fortification. Although the Cape Fear River was more than a mile wide at that point, low bluffs overlooked the river's narrow chan-

After repulsing the 1748 Spanish attack on their town, Brunswick residents salvaged this portrait of Jesus Christ with the crown of thorns from the captain's cabin of the derelict Spanish sloop *Fortuna* in the Cape Fear River. *St. James Church*

On March 23, 1862, Brig. Gen. Samuel Gibbs French ordered "the construction of a battery and line of entrenchments" at Brunswick Point. *U.S. Army Military History Institute*

General French was determined to meet the threat by building additional strong forts around Wilmington. Upon his return to headquarters, French instructed Lt. Thomas Rowland to "superintend the construction of a battery and line of entrenchments" at Brunswick. Rowland was well qualified for the assignment. As a Cadet of Engineers in the Confederate States Army, he had been supervising the construction of batteries and mounting artillery at Fort Johnston in Smithville since October 1861. The young officer had accompanied General French and his staff on the survey trip of the Cape Fear defenses, during which he favorably impressed the new district commander as an "educated, accomplished soldier of uncommon intelligence." This accomplished soldier was, in fact, a cadet fresh out of the United States Military Academy at West Point. The young lieutenant was indeed possessed of uncommon intelligence. He had ranked first in his academy class in math and English, and studied military engineering. He resigned from West Point near the end of his sophomore year when Virginia seceeded from the Union.

Despite his Northern birth, Rowland desired to serve in the army of his adopted home state. He quickly received a commission as a second lieutenant in the Provisional Army of Virginia from Governor John Letcher on May 4, 1861, and ten weeks later, on July 12, Rowland was appointed by Confederate authorities a cadet in the Corps of Engineers. In October 1861, Lieutenant Rowland was sent to southeastern North Carolina to help build fortifications for Wilmington's protection. All in all, he spent nine months in the Lower Cape Fear overseeing military projects. During that time, Rowland's most important assignment was constructing a fortification at "Brunswick Point."

Acting on General French's orders, Rowland returned to Brunswick to begin construction on March 24, 1862, just one day shy of his twentieth birthday. The birthday boy took up resi-

nel, which ran within a few yards of the west bank. A battery on the high ground, French believed, would command both the river traffic and the western land approaches to Wilmington. The city needed these fortifications to stem the tide of Federal forces steadily advancing down the North Carolina coast. After capturing Forts Hatteras and Clark on the state's Outer Banks in late August 1861, Union naval and expeditionary forces moved into Pamlico and Albemarle sounds. In February 1862, they overran Roanoke Island, a hinge on the backdoor to Richmond, before turning southward. On March 14, the Federals captured New Bern, only ninety miles north of Wilmington. The supposition among the Cape Fear's Confederate military authorities was that Wilmington was the enemy's next target.[7]

Adjoining Fort Anderson's Battery B is Lt. Thomas Rowland's original six-foot high earthen wall that runs westward for a mile to Orton Pond. Confederate infantry and field artillery covered this front. *Author's Collection*

vants to Rowland and his aides while they worked on their project. "The gentleman who owns the plantation gives us the use of his home, and servants to cook for us and wait upon us," Lieutenant Rowland explained. "He is a lawyer and spends most of his time in Wilmington, so we have the whole house to ourselves."[8]

Each morning Rowland and his craftsmen walked down to Brunswick to work on the defenses. In the following five weeks, the young lieutenant laid off and supervised the construction of an artillery battery near the Cape Fear River adjoined by a six-foot high wall of dirt that ran westward for almost a mile to a huge mill lake called Orton Pond. Slaves hired from farms and plantations throughout the southeastern part of the Old North State, as well as some free blacks, performed most of the hard labor. With their arrival beginning on or about April 10, 1862, Tarheel

dence at Orton, an imposing colonial rice plantation one mile-and-a-half north of Old Brunswick, along with "master-carpenter" George W. Rose and a "master-workman," either Robert B. Wood or his brother John C. Wood. Orton Plantation's 9,026-acre tract included Brunswick, on which Rowland planned to build his fort. Orton's wartime landlord, Thomas C. Miller, Jr., generously loaned his house and ser-

Had a photographer visited Fort St. Philip in 1863, he might well have "captured the likeness" of a scene similar to this one showing black laborers clearing the fort's ramparts 100 years later. Slaves and free blacks performed much of the hard work in constructing the earthwork defenses. *Brunswick Town State Historic Site*

soldiers supplemented Brunswick's workforce of black laborers. Captain Calvin Barnes' Company Unattached North Carolina Artillery (later designated 2nd Company H, 40th Regiment North Carolina Troops) and Captain Alexander MacRae's Company Heavy Artillery (later known as Company C, 1st Battalion North Carolina Heavy Artillery) comprised the first garrison troops at the Brunswick bastion. These units were joined by Capt. John E. Leggett's Company C, 40th Regiment N.C. Troops.[9]

The massive brick shell of St. Philip's Anglican Church, the only remaining structure of the colonial town of Brunswick, stands just inside the earthen walls of Confederate Fort Anderson. *Author's Collection*

Not until the Brunswick fort was attacked in the war's last winter did a larger contingent of men live and work inside its walls than in the spring and summer of 1862. For a time, perhaps as many as 300 gray-uniformed men toiled in

Lieutenant Thomas Rowland and his "master craftsmen" bunked at the Orton Plantation mansion as they began construction on the Brunswick Point defenses in the spring of 1862. *Orton Plantation*

tandem with the force of black laborers clearing the woods, digging trenches, and piling up dirt for the fort's ramparts, one shovel full at a time. They also erected bombproof shelters, barracks and storehouses using ballast stones and bricks salvaged from the colonial ruins for the new buildings' footings, piers, and chimneys.

The fort's construction was strenuous work made even more difficult, as summer approached, by the increasing heat and humidity, pesky mosquitoes, deer flies, and sand gnats (called no-see-ums because of their tiny size). Alligators that filled the area's abundant freshwater ponds and creeks, and poisonous snakes made the job even hazardous at times. "All this country about here is interspersed with ponds and marshes. The ponds are well stocked with fish and alligators," observed a Confederate officer. "One of the soldiers shot an alligator the other day with his musket. Their skin is so tough that it is difficult to kill them. I shot one

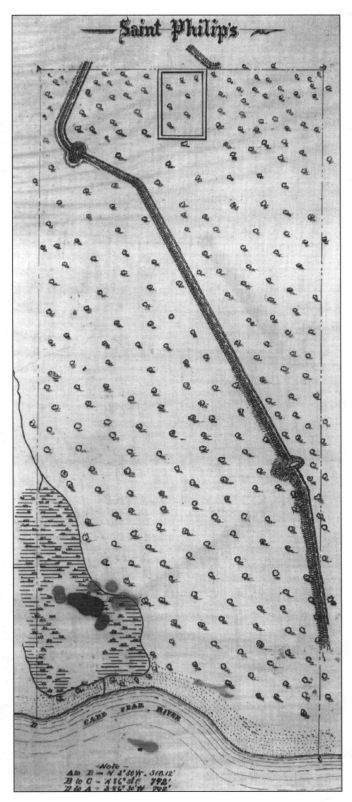

"I am spending a day or two in [Wilmington]," Lt. Thomas Rowland wrote to his mother on June 18, 1862. "I came up on Monday to get a transit and some mathematical instruments to make a survey and a map of Fort St. Philip and the Line of Intrenchments adjoining it." *Author's Collection*

with a rifle, but the ball glanced off his back without hurting him."

Despite the obstacles he and his workers faced, Lieutenant Rowland reported on April 25, 1862, that he had "nearly finished the Line of Intrenchments. . .extending from the Battery on the river to a pond [six] miles in length." According to Rowland's wartime correspondence, Capt. Boyd Edelin was the first commander of the battery. The adjacent line of earthworks cut through the middle of Brunswick Town, abutting the remains of the old courthouse, homes, and St. Philip's Church. Rowland covered as many of the buildings' foundations and crumbled chimneys with his dirt walls as he could, fearing that the brick and ballast stones might become a hailstorm of life-threatening debris if hit by enemy artillery shells.

The surviving brick shell of St. Philip's Church was left untouched and even inspired the fort's original name. "On our line of defenses is an old church. . .of the Parish in old colonial days, and has already witnessed the struggles of one revolution," noted Thomas Rowland. "We think of calling our battery Fort St. Philip." The suggestion became official on May 11, 1862, when Maj. William Lamb christened the works Fort St. Philip, in tribute to the "silent witness to the successful struggle of our fathers for liberty and independence."[10]

Major Lamb was one of the fathers' sons struggling for Southern independence and the Brunswick bastion's second commandant. An aristocratic lawyer and newspaper editor from Norfolk, Virginia, Lamb had come to the Wilmington area in September 1861 as chief quartermaster on the staff of fellow Virginian Brig. Gen. Joseph Reid Anderson, the first Richmond-appointed commander of the District of the Cape Fear. When Anderson's reassignment as commander of the Department of North Carolina in mid-March 1862 sent him to

"A fine, dashing young Confederate officer," Maj. William Lamb christened the Brunswick defenses Fort St. Philip on May 11, 1862. Soon thereafter, Lamb was transferred to command at Fort Fisher across the Cape Fear River. *Courtesy of William Lamb*

Goldsboro, Lamb remained behind in Wilmington.

Anderson's successor, Brig. Gen. Samuel Gibbs French, may have initially sent quartermaster Major Lamb to feed, clothe, and equip the first wave of garrison troops that reached Brunswick in the spring of 1862. But the intelligent young officer's organizational and leadership skills could not be overlooked, and on or about May 4, 1862, Lamb was assigned as the Brunswick post commandant. The twenty-six-year old major was well liked and respected by both his superiors and subordinates. "I wish you could know him," wrote an admirer, "he is a Christian and a gentleman as well as a soldier." Another devotee said that "Lamb was one of the most lovable men in existence, a fine, dashing young Confederate officer." The young officer's popularity among the troops got him elected colonel of the 36th Regiment North Carolina Troops (2nd Regiment North Carolina Artillery) on May 14, 1862. Flying atop Lamb's headquarters at Fort St. Philip was a flag bearing the

motto: "Pace cives–bello milites (citizen's in peace—soldier's in war)."[11]

As a "soldier in war," William Lamb was enthralled with fortification construction. He studied books on the subject and probably learned the art first hand from Thomas Rowland at Fort St. Philip. Lamb and Rowland became fast friends, in part because of their common interest in military engineering and because they were both Virginians. When Lamb assumed the colonelcy of the 36th North Carolina, he requested that Rowland be assigned as his adjutant, a position the young engineer filled, unofficially at least, until both officers were transferred to other commands. On July 4, 1862, Lamb was reassigned to command at Fort Fisher on the east side of the Cape Fear River, while Rowland was transferred shortly thereafter to Virginia, where he served as assistant adjutant general to Brig. Gen. Robert Ransom for the remainder of the war. Even after their separation, however, Lamb and Rowland kept in touch, recalling in their correspondence their association at Fort St. Philip.

With Lamb's departure, temporary command of the Brunswick fort passed to the second ranking officer of the newly formed 36th North Carolina Regiment, Lt. Col. John A. Richardson. Extant records do not indicate how long Richardson remained commandant. He was still in command at Fort St. Philip on September 19, 1862, two and a half months after Lamb had left. Richardson's successor at Brunswick was probably Maj. John Jackson Hedrick, also of the 36th North Carolina. Hedrick was in command at the fort by May 1863, was still in command the following August, and probably remained in command at St. Philip until his promotion to colonel of the 40th North Carolina (3rd Regiment North Carolina Artillery) on December 1, 1863.[12]

While details of his tenure at Fort St. Philip are sketchy, John Hedrick was well known in the Lower Cape Fear long before he assumed the head position at Brunswick. Before the war

Hedrick worked as a salesman in the dry goods store of John Dawson (Wilmington's wartime mayor). An ardent secessionist, Hedrick helped organize and then commanded the Cape Fear Minute Men, a militia unit comprised of Southern nationalists. During the height of the disunion crisis in January 1861, Captain Hedrick's Cape Fear Minute Men took possession of U.S. Forts Johnston at Smithville and

Caswell on Oak Island at the mouth of the Cape Fear River. Although North Carolina Governor John W. Ellis immediately returned the forts to Federal authorities, Hedrick's brash action made him a hero among the region's Confederate zealots.

Even before North Carolina joined the Confederacy, Hedrick began enrolling men in a new unit, the Cape Fear Light Artillery. Later designated 1st Company C, 36th Regiment North Carolina Troops, Captain Hedrick's unit served during the war in various forts and batteries along the state's coastal plain, including Fort Fisher. Hedrick commanded at Fort Fisher from late January 1862 until July 4 of that year, when Col. William Lamb assumed command. The recently commissioned Major Hedrick was then transferred to other forts and batteries in the Lower Cape Fear, including Fort St. Philip, before being sent in the late autumn of 1863 to command on Bald Head Island, where he helped plan and construct Fort Holmes to guard Old Inlet.[13]

During his reign at Brunswick Point, Hedrick strengthened and expanded the earthwork defenses. Fort St. Philip also underwent another important change during Hedrick's administration: it was renamed. In accordance with Maj. Gen. William Henry Chase Whiting's General Orders No. 33 of July 1, 1863, several Cape Fear forts and batteries

A well known Wilmington dry goods salesman and militia officer before the war, Maj. John Jackson Hedrick (in a previously unpublished view) strengthened and expanded the Brunswick bastion during his tenure as commander there in 1863. *Author's Collection*

Major General W.H.C. Whiting
U.S. Army Military History Institute

NEW ADVERTISEMENTS.

HEAD QUART'RS DISTRICT CAPE FEAR,
WILMINGTON, N. C., July 1st, 1863.

GENERAL ORDERS
No. 33.

I. TO COMMEMORATE some of the many distinguished and gallant dead of North Carolina, who have given their lives for their country, the names of the following of the Forts and Batteries of the Cape Fear, will be changed, viz :

Fort Johnson will be known hereafter as Ft. Branch.
Fort St. Phillip,   "   "   "   " Ft. Anderson.
Fort Hill,   "   "   "   " Ft. Meares.
Ft. Gun Battery   "   "   "   " Ft. Campbell.
Fort French,   "   "   "   " Ft. Lee.
Fort Strong,   "   "   "   " Ft. Davis.
Battery Tirza,   "   "   "   " Battery Stokes.

The remaining batteries on the river will not be designated at present, otherwise than by numbers as heretofore, except five, on the city front, which, commencing with the lowest, will be known after some brave sons of Willmington as follows :

Battery WRIGHT.
"   MEARES,
"   MOORE,
"   VANBOKKELEN,
"   COWAN.

By command of

Maj. Gen'l WHITING.
JAS. H. HILL,
Maj. & A. A. Gen'l.

July 2, 1863.   225-1t.

Cape Fear District commander Maj. Gen. W.H.C. Whiting issued General Orders No. 33 that changed the name of Fort St. Philip to Fort Anderson. The military notice ran in the *Wilmington Daily Journal* for only one day–July 2, 1863. *Wilmington Daily Journal*

underwent name changes to "commemorate some of the many distinguished and gallant dead of North Carolina, who have given their lives for their country." Fort St. Philip was to "be known hereafter" as Fort Anderson.[14]

Historians have long assumed, and with good reason, that Fort Anderson was named for Brig. Gen. Joseph Reid Anderson, who was most noted for being president of the Tredegar Iron Works in Richmond, the largest supplier of Confederate ordnance products. He was also the first Richmond-appointed commander of the District of the Cape Fear, whose good service in the region between early September 1861 and March 15, 1862, was indeed acknowledged by the local military authorities. Battery Anderson, an artillery position erected along the ocean shoreline two miles north of Fort Fisher on Federal Point, was named for Joseph Reid Anderson. Erroneous information provided many years after the war, however, led to the mistaken identity of Fort Anderson's namesake.

Interested in commemorating the history of Fort Anderson, after the war, the New Hanover Historical Commission requested advice from Eugene S. Martin, a former lieutenant of Company A, 1st Battalion North Carolina Heavy Artillery, who had served a brief stint at the Brunswick bastion in early 1865 and was one of the Lower Cape Fear's last surviving Confederate veterans. In a letter dated November 6, 1919, Martin informed Rev. Andrew J. Howell, chairman of the historical board, that Fort Anderson was "begun in 1861 and named in honor of General Joseph R. Anderson, then commanding the military district." Armed with that information, the commission installed a handsome marble plaque, that quoted Martin's statement almost verba-

tim, at the base of St. Philip's Church. Historical records now show that Eugene S. Martin was mistaken about Fort Anderson. The wartime correspondence of Thomas Rowland, Fort Anderson's original architect, noted that construction on the Brunswick stronghold did not begin until late March 1862. It also appears that Martin was unaware of, or had forgotten about, General Orders No. 33, wherein General Whiting ordered that Fort Anderson's name would commemorate the "distinguished and gallant dead of North Carolina." That requirement alone proves that Fort Anderson could not have been named for Joseph Reid Anderson, who was a Virginian very much alive at the time Whiting issued his directive.[15]

More than likely, the "distinguished and gallant dead of North Carolina" for whom Fort Anderson was named was Brig. Gen. George Burgwyn Anderson, the only Tarheel general officer with that surname. Although originally from Hillsboro, North Carolina, Anderson was a descendant of one of the Cape Fear's oldest families, and a grand nephew of John Burgwyn, an early leading planter and merchant of the region. Despite the agricultural and entrepreneurial pursuits of his great uncle, George B.

Anderson became a military man by trade—a graduate of West Point and a lieutenant of dragoons in the U.S. Army, before he resigned his commission to become colonel of the 4th North Carolina Infantry when the Civil War broke out. Considered

Historians have long, but mistakenly, assumed that Fort Anderson was named for Brig. Gen. Joseph Reid Anderson of Virginia, who served as the first Richmond appointed commander of the Cape Fear District. Anderson was most noted for being president of Richmond's Tredegar Iron Works, the largest supplier of Confederate ordnance products. *U.S. Army Military History Institute*

Fort Anderson was most likely named for North Carolina Brig. Gen. George Burgwyn Anderson, who was a direct descendant of one of the Lower Cape Fear's oldest families. Wounded while commanding his troops at the Battle of Sharpsburg in September 1862, General Anderson died shortly thereafter. The Cape Fear District commander paid homage to George B. Anderson by renaming the Confederate fort at Brunswick in his honor. *N.C. Division of Archives and History*

a "furious fighter," Anderson received a battlefield promotion as brigadier general after impressing President Jefferson Davis with his nerve and leadership at the Battle of Williamsburg in the spring of 1862. He went on to lead his brigade in combat at Malvern Hill, South Mountain, and Sharpsburg. While commanding his troops in the "Bloody Lane" at Sharpsburg, General Anderson was struck by a bullet in the right foot. Though not considered a life-threatening wound at first, it soon became infected and required amputation of his foot. Anderson never recovered and died in Raleigh on October 16, 1862.[16]

Work on the Cape Fear fort ultimately named in George Burgwyn Anderson's honor continued for almost three years. By the time the Brunswick stronghold was completed it was the Cape Fear's most powerful interior defensive work, and second in size and strength only to mighty Fort Fisher on the opposite side of the river. To reach that status, however, Fort Anderson underwent a major metamorphosis, such that Lt. Thomas Rowland's 1862 work was barely recognizeable when it was finally attacked three years later.

From the riverside, Fort Anderson was shaped like a huge crooked letter L, with the short end running parallel to the Cape Fear River and the long shank running perpendicular to the waterway. The fort's main strength was its eastern anchor along the river's edge. Rowland's old redoubt built close to the river was transformed into an impressive twenty-four-foot-high crescent-shaped bastion, designated Battery B on Union maps. Located at the rough intersection of the L's two shanks, the imposing bastion was pitted with five gun chambers, each containing a 6.4-inch, 32-pounder cannon pointing downriver. The guns were mounted on thick wooden carriages en barbette (to fire over the top of the

By February 1865, Fort Anderson's armament comprised nine 6.4-inch, 32-pounder seacoast guns mounted on heavy wooden carriages en barbette, similar to the 1829 pattern 32-pounder pictured here. *Author's Collection*

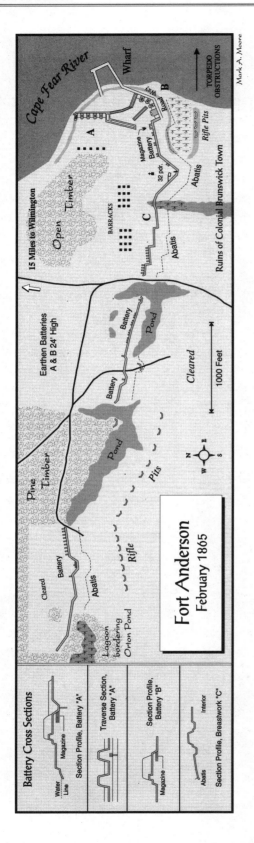

Fort Anderson
February 1865

Mark A. Moore

From a birdseye view, Fort Anderson looked like a huge crooked letter L, with the short end hugging the edge of the Cape Fear River and the long shank snaking westward for a mile to Orton Pond. Begun in 1862, Fort Anderson was built atop the colonial ghost town of Brunswick, England's main port of entry in North Carolina before the American Revolution. The fort's main strength was its eastern anchor along the shoreline. Two massive twenty-four foot high artillery batteries mounting nine seacoast guns guarded the river channel. Abutting the main fort's west flank was a six-foot high earthen wall designed to accomodate both infantry and field artillery.

For the better part of three years, slaves, free blacks and Confederate soldiers labored on the fort. By the time Union naval and ground forces attacked it in February 1865, Fort Anderson was the largest and strongest interior fortification in the Lower Cape Fear. As imposing as the fort appeared, it had one weakness: its right (inland) flank was open and subject to a turning movement.

fort), and were separated by a large mound of dirt called a traverse, which stood slightly higher than the crest, or parapet, of the fort. Traverses were designed to protect cannon and crew from enfilading fire, so that if a shell exploded in one gun chamber, soldiers and artillery in an adjacent chamber would be protected from flying shrapnel and debris. Built underneath at least some of the traverses were ordnance magazines for storing gunpowder and artillery projectiles, or bombproofs where soldiers could take refuge during a bombardment.

The short end of the L was a huge 150-yard long artillery emplacement constructed just north of Battery B. Called Battery A, it ran parallel to the Cape Fear River and guarded against any attempt by enemy vessels to ascend the waterway. Like Battery B, the walls of Battery A averaged about twenty-four feet in height, were interspersed with five gun chambers separated by traverses, and sodded with grass to prevent erosion. Battery A also boasted 6.4-inch, 32-pounder guns. While the U.S. Army's *Official Military Atlas* map of Fort Anderson designates these earthworks Battery A and Battery B, that probably reflects Union nomenclature and not the original Confederate names of the batteries, which are unknown. The batteries were linked in a disjointed fashion by three sand walls, two of which were similar in size and appearance to Batteries A and B, but they did not contain artillery compartments.

Abutting Battery B's west flank was Thomas Rowland's original six-foot high earthen wall with a series of small emplacements added for light artillery. One 32-pounder cannon was also mounted along this line at St. Philip's Church, which was located just inside the fort's walls. From this point the earthen line extended about a mile to the east end of Orton Pond. Buoyed mines (called "torpedoes" in those days), pilings and stone-filled cribs in the river complemented the fort's defenses.[17]

The soldiers who built the powerful earthworks at Brunswick expressed pride in their accomplishment. In a letter to the editor of the *Wilmington Journal* printed on May 28, 1863, one anonymous artillerymen of Company E, 36th North Carolina Regiment boasted:

> We have at length, by the sweat of our brows, and the power of our bone and muscle, completed one of the most formidable batteries in the Southern Confederacy. Guided and sustained by the energy and perseverance of Major [John J.] Hedrick, commanding (who is a good commander and a gentlemen to boot), we have put up a work which will compare favourably with any work of its kind in the country, and now only want certain additions to our armament to feel confident of being able to defy all Yankeedom to reach Wilmington by this route. We have, up to this time, done our full duty in building fortifications for the defense of Wilmington, as well as for the protection of our homes and firesides, our wives and children, and of most of all near and dear to us. If the enemy should ever approach us here, we intend to give him a warm reception. With the help of God, we intend to stand by our guns until the last man falls, or gain the victory.[18]

After making an inspection of the Lower Cape Fear defenses, Gen. W. H. C. Whiting, who was assigned district commander in November 1862, reported that "Battery Saint Philip [was] well constructed." His praise notwithstanding, General Whiting (who was considered one of the best engineers in the Confederacy), still found the fort "defective in the quality and caliber of its ordnance." The garrison had requisitioned rifled cannon of heavy caliber, but most of the coveted big seacoast guns were placed in Forts Fisher, Caswell, and Holmes guarding the inlets, leaving Fort Anderson to settle for antiquated weapons. Whiting recognized the weakness, but the 32-pounder guns were all he could procur for the fort from the ordnance authorities. Hopefully, it would be enough.[19]

From the twenty-four-foot high summit of Battery B, visitors can fully appreciate the size, strength and features of Confederate Fort Anderson. Looking in a southwestwardly direction, the battery's gun chambers and traverses are as clearly defined today as they were in 1865.   *Courtesy of Jerry Netherland*

Looking northward from behind Battery B, the still imposing remains of Fort Anderson's Battery A loom in the background. Artillery in Battery A guarded against enemy vessels attempting to ascend the Cape Fear River, as seen through the trees. *Courtesy of Jerry Netherland*

Scarce documentation provides little glimpse into the day-to-day activities of the common Confederate soldier stationed at Fort St. Philip—Fort Anderson. Garrison life there compared to garrison life at most forts, with soldiers engaged in regular, tedious, monotonous duties occasionally interrupted by some distraction or mild excitement. The soldiers' daily routine at the Brunswick bastion included laboring on the earthworks, constructing barracks and other buildings, and constant drilling on the heavy and light artillery. All in all it was a boring existence. "I think this is the dullest life I ever led," complained one Confederate soldier. "In my experience in the field there was always something to keep up a pleasant state of excitement, but here, there is neither the march nor the anticipation of a fight to cause our blood to move hurriedly through our veins."[20]

An isolated post, the Brunswick position saw none of the hustle and bustle associated with wartime Wilmington, or even the village of Smithville. For most of the war, Anderson's soldiers did not wage any engagement with enemy troops or duel with enemy blockading ships, unlike their comrades at Forts Fisher and Caswell. With the exception of Orton Plantation just north of the fort, Fort Anderson was far removed from civilian residences. "This is a very bleak place we are at," commented one of the fort's defenders. Incoming blockade runners and mail packets stopped at Anderson's docks on a regular basis, but contact with outsiders was otherwise infrequent, leaving the garrison feeling abandoned and disregarded. "We have been neglected in toto," lamented one frustrated soldier in the Clarendon Artillery. "Our mind leads us home to our relatives and friends, and the society of loved ones. But alas! we are here [at Fort St. Philip] deprived of the enjoyments of other days." An artilleryman of Company E, 36th North Carolina echoed similar sentiments: "We have suffered the severest hardships and privations that soldiers could do to be stationed in a garrison."[21]

The deprivation and isolation took their toll on the soldiers, some of whom chose to desert their post. On June 21, 1862, less than three months after being stationed at Fort St. Philip, Privates Arnold C. Congleton, James Henry Congleton and William S. Congleton of Company C, 40th North Carolina, went absent without leave. The Congleton boys were joined in flight by Privates John B. McMahon and William John Philly, all of whom lived in Beaufort County and may have attempted to make their way home.

Other than bothersome insects during the hot months (and boredom and loneliness), camp diseases were the soldiers' biggest enemies at Brunswick. A variety of ailments drove seventeen-year-old Pvt. Paul Lesesne out of the army. A former student from Bladen County, North Carolina, Private Lesesne enlisted in

"This is a very bleak place we are at..."

Capt. Calvin Barnes' Company Unattached North Carolina Artillery on May 26, 1862. Two months later he was discharged "by reasons of general debility, having had measles, dysentery, and remittent fever." Obviously, Private Lesesne did not take to army life. Private Horatio Babson of Company E, 36th North Carolina was not so fortunate: he died of disease at Fort St. Philip on October 26, 1862.[22]

For those men who endured the camp diseases, desolation and dull duty, however, garrison life presented few serious problems and even offered some benefits not enjoyed by soldiers in the field. Off-duty time at Fort Anderson allowed soldiers to explore and hunt in the vast piney woods surrounding the fort, fish in the Cape Fear River and Orton Pond, or wander about the ghostly remains of Old Brunswick. In excavating the earth for the fort's batteries, the diggers uncovered coins, buttons and other assorted relics from the vanished colonial town. One gunner in the Clarendon Artillery expressed his relative contentment on being stationed at Fort St. Philip: "Happily we are stationed near the great deep," he wrote. "Sometimes while treading our weary path as a sentinel. . .and while the stillness of the night rests upon all around, our mind is attracted by the [distant] thundering of the mighty ocean [and] we then reflect upon the safety of our camp."[23]

For the fort-bound soldiers, the hardships and privations were eased by letters and packages from loved ones back home. Family news, mementos and home-cooked food, all of which were eagerly awaited, provided the men with great pleasure amid the isolation and tedium of life at Fort Anderson. "I was so glad to hear from

you and all my friends. . .it was the next thing to seeing you," wrote Pvt. Archibald D. McEwen of the Bladen Artillery Guards to his wife in Bladen County. McEwen also mentioned that he had nothing "interesting or satisfactory" to say, except that he wanted "to get home mighty bad." After receiving a letter from his mother, one of McEwen's comrades noted that he was "much cheered by the perusal of it, continue to write me fully and frequently."[24]

To combat the soldiers' feelings of neglect, the local military authorities regularly transferred troops in and out of Fort Anderson. With too few troops to protect the Cape Fear District at any given time, most of the defenders were stationed at what the high command considered more vulnerable points along the oceanfront where the enemy might come ashore. "Our force at Fort St. Philip has been but limited ever since the post was established," claimed one gray-clad soldier. Another suggested that "a kind Minister to visit our hospital and give a word of encouragement to the poor soldier," would help ease their discomfort at Fort St. Philip. Yet another comrade believed that a garrison flag would encourage pride and mitigate frustration among the disaffected soldiers. "Our beautiful flagstaff is without a flag," he wrote in September 1862. "Cannot the citizens of Wilmington, especially the ladies, supply us with one?"[25]

In addition to its status as a formidable defensive position, Fort St. Philip—Fort Anderson also served as a camp of muster, where young men enlisted in a military company "for the war." Most of the enlistees were local boys from the surrounding eight counties that comprised the District of the Cape Fear: New Hanover, Brunswick, Bladen, Columbus, Onslow, Sampson, Robeson, and Cumberland. Captain George Tait's Company North Carolina Volunteers (later designated 2nd Company K [Bladen Artillery Guards], 40th Regiment North Carolina Troops) organized in Bladen County, but was mustered into service at Fort St. Philip

Lt. Oliver H. Powell served in Company E, 36th North Carolina Troops (2nd N.C. Artillery) at Fort St. Philip during the summer of 1862. *Walter Clark, North Carolina Regiments*

on May 15, 1862. In early August 1863, the *Wilmington Journal* printed Capt. John E. Leggett's advertisement looking for recruits to join Company C, 40th North Carolina Regiment then stationed at Fort Anderson. "Had [you] selected from all of North Carolina's soldiery, [you] could not have formed a Regiment better chosen for the defense of its sea-coast," Lt. Col. John A. Richardson of the 36th North Carolina pointed out to Governor Zebulon B. Vance concerning the garrison. "We are Cape Fear men, sir, 'native, and to the manner born.' Our homes, and the blue waters that wash their thresholds, are here."[26]

One major responsibility of these "Cape Fear men" was the management of Fort Anderson as a quarantine station. Every Wilmington-bound blockade runner that entered the harbor was required to stop at the Brunswick bastion to be checked for proper manifest papers, illegal cargoes ("Yankee goods") and contagious diseases. The establishment of Fort Anderson as a quarantine station was prompted in part by a devastating yellow fever epidemic that claimed 654 victims in Wilmington alone during the autumn of 1862. Survivors believed that the blockade runner *Kate* had inadvertently imported the pestilence from Nassau. To curb such tragedies, Fort Anderson's inspectors carefully monitored each incoming blockade runner.

Despite the risks, Lt. Charles S. Powell of Company B, 10th Battalion North Carolina Heavy Artillery, liked serving as an inspector at Fort St. Philip. "We did quarantine duty here, all incoming vessels were detained a few days," Powell recalled. "It was a great pleasure for the inspecting officer (of which I was one) to board the vessels for examination. They had tropical fruits of which they were very liberal with, as well as some refreshments." Perhaps the refreshments and other gifts Powell and his comrades received from blockade running agents expedited the inspection process at Fort Anderson.[27]

Even if that was the case, the fort's inspectors were still accountable for the quarantine regulations, as well as the security of all property landed from the ships. No ship passed without undergoing scrutiny by officials onshore, even if that meant forcing vessels to stop. Purser's clerk James Sprunt reported that a blockade runner on which he was serving was brought to a sudden halt off Fort Anderson:

> While passing Fort Anderson, a gun was fired, but having received no intimation at Fort Fisher that we would be detained on the river, we continued our course, which was immediately arrested by another gun sending a round through our rigging. We were boarded by Lieutenant McNair (still known as crazy Mac) who laughingly remarked that his next shot would have sunk us, as his orders were to stop all vessels passing the fort, for inspection.[28]

Not until the vessels were cleared by the fort's resident inspectors were they allowed to proceed upriver to Wilmington's docks. How long those docks would be available to receive supplies from overseas, however, concerned Confederate authorities.

Chapter 2

The Threat

Union warships unleashed the largest bombardment of the war on Fort Fisher, in an effort to weaken the defenses for a ground assault by U.S. soldiers, sailors and marines on January 15, 1865. *Battle and Leaders of the Civil War*

Union efforts to seal Wilmington to blockade running were a long time coming, despite the fact that the U.S. Navy had targeted the city as early as the summer of 1861. It was then that the Union Blockade Strategy Board had recommended striking the seaport while its defenses were still relatively weak. The Cape Fear's shoal waters, however, made a purely naval attack impractical, since warships could not get close enough to shore to destroy the growing number of Confederate forts and batteries. The navy insisted that Wilmington could only be captured by a carefully planned and executed combined army-navy operation. The U.S. Army and the Lincoln administration, however, had other priorities, most notably the capture of Richmond. Wilmington would have to wait.

The Navy Department intensified its efforts to gain the War Department's support for an attack on Wilmington in the spring of 1862. While inertia plagued the Army of the Potomac

in Virginia early that year, the U.S. Navy experienced considerable success along the South's coast. Between March and May, naval and expeditionary forces captured six of the Confederacy's principal seaports: Fernandina, Jacksonville, and Pensacola, Florida; New Bern, North Carolina; New Orleans, Louisiana; and Norfolk, Virginia. In addition, Savannah, Georgia was effectively sealed off from blockade running when Fort Pulaski fell in April.

With momentum tilting in his favor, U.S. Navy Secretary Gideon Welles proposed a movement against Wilmington in May, but his plan received little attention as the Army of the Potomac, led by Maj. Gen. George B. McClellan, finally advanced on Richmond. After the failure of McClellan's Peninsula Campaign that summer and the reorganization of the army's high command that autumn, Welles renewed his efforts against Wilmington. He prepared a diversionary attack at the Cape Fear to coincide with a revived plan to invade Virginia by the army's new commander, Maj. Gen. Ambrose E. Burnside. The navy assembled a force of iron-clads (including the famed *Monitor*) for a thrust on Wilmington through Old Inlet, while Union ground forces were poised to strike the city from New Bern. The advance disintergrated, however, when Burnside's army was thrashed by Robert E. Lee at Fredericksburg in mid-December 1862, and the *Monitor*, en route to Wilmington, sank in a storm off Cape Hatteras, North Carolina, on New Year's Eve 1862.

Acting Rear Admiral S. Phillips Lee proposed several ideas for taking Wilmington . . .

During the next two years, Acting Rear Admiral S. Phillips Lee, commander of the North Atlantic Blockading Squadron, proposed several ideas for taking Wilmington, but to no avail. The army showed no interest in providing a large expeditionary force to strike a seaport it considered of little strategic value. With no army support and limited resources at its disposal, the U.S. Navy was forced to pick and choose its targets. Attention shifted away from Wilmington to Charleston, South Carolina, where the war had begun with the attack on Fort Sumter, and where popular and political interests centered. Combined operations on the Mississippi River also took precedence. All the while, blockade runners smuggled in tons of supplies and provisions for the Confederacy by way of Wilmington. "To close the port of Wilmington is undoubtedly the most important and effective demonstration that can be made," Gideon Welles cogently argued. "If of less prestige than the capture of Richmond, it would be

as damaging to the Rebels." Unfortunately for the navy chief, the War Department did not agree.[1]

Finally, in the summer of 1864, the government's attitude toward Wilmington changed. By late August, Rear Admiral David G. Farragut had captured the forts guarding the entrance to Mobile Bay, Alabama, and sealed off the harbor, leaving Wilmington as the only major Confederate seaport open to the outside world. Secretary Welles used Farragut's victory to convince President Abraham Lincoln of the importance of going after the North Carolina port. This time Lincoln concurred, recognizing that the city's fall would not only sever the Confederacy's lifeline, but pacify Northern shippers who were pressuring the administration to combat Wilmington-based commerce raiders. The seaport's capture might also reap some political benefits for the president by bolstering his sputtering campaign for reelection that autumn. Although Lincoln endorsed Welles' proposal to attack Wilmington, he deferred final approval to Lt. Gen. Ulysses S. Grant.

Initially, General Grant expressed little enthusiasm for committing an expeditionary force for the attack. In his opinion, he needed more soldiers, not fewer, to keep the pressure on Robert E. Lee. Since the spring of 1864, Grant's operational forces—the Army of the Potomac and the Army of the James—had Lee's army bottlenecked between Petersburg and Richmond. The commanding Union general did not believe he could afford to spare the estimated 10,000 troops for an amphibious assault 240 miles away on the North Carolina coast. Repeated frontal assaults against Lee's vastly undermanned but strongly entrenched Army of Northern Virginia (followed by equally unsuccessful efforts to outflank his defenses) gained little, and Grant had been unable to break the deadlock. Welles argued, however, that the Virginia deadlock could be broken by sealing the last gateway that blockade runners continued to use to bring in food, clothing, and weapons for Lee's beleaguered forces.

Grant finally came around, agreeing to supply the navy with army troops for the Wilmington expedition by October. Despite the commanding general's assurances, however, it was not until December that the expeditionary force was given the go-ahead to proceed to Hampton Roads, Virginia, to link-up with the navy, which had been prepared to sail two months earlier. Sixty-four warships, the largest fleet assembled during the war, finally advanced southward on December 13.[2]

Commanding the great armada was Rear Admiral David D. Porter, an authoritative, ambitious and acerbic fifty-one year-old veteran. A scion of sailors, Porter had won his laurels fighting along the Mississippi River, where he quickly emerged as one of the navy's brightest and most successful executive officers. He had directed a mortar flotilla at the capture of New Orleans in April 1862, and six months later, as commander of the Mississippi Squadron, had helped take Arkansas Post and thereafter Vicksburg in 1863. The capture of Vicksburg, which U.S. Grant professed "could not have been successfully made" without the navy's willing assistance, helped Porter win a promotion to

rear admiral and head of the entire Mississippi River system. He remained in that position until ordered east to take command of the North Atlantic Blockading Squadron in October 1864. After carefully considering other worthy candidates, Gideon Welles concluded that Porter was "the best man for the service" of capturing the Confederacy's last major seaport.[3]

To complement Porter's naval effort, General Grant assigned Maj. Gen. Godfrey Weitzel, former chief engineer of the Army of the James, to command a 6,500-man expeditionary force from the newly formed XXIV and XXV Army Corps. Weitzel's instructions called for him to assist the navy in closing down Wilmington to blockade running by capturing Fort Fisher, which guarded New Inlet, the blockade runners' favorite entrance into the Cape Fear harbor. Much to Grant's and Porter's chagrin, Weitzel's superior, Maj. Gen. Benjamin F. Butler, decided to accompany the expedition, and, in effect, take over army command.

There was bad blood between Porter and Butler going back to New Orleans in 1862, where they had argued over Porter's role in the city's capture. In short, they did not like each other. The acrimonious relationship between the two service branch commanders did not instill General

Confident, conceited and capable, Rear Admiral David D. Porter was considered the "best man for the service" of capturing Wilmington, the Confederacy's last major blockade running seaport. *Aurthor's Collection*

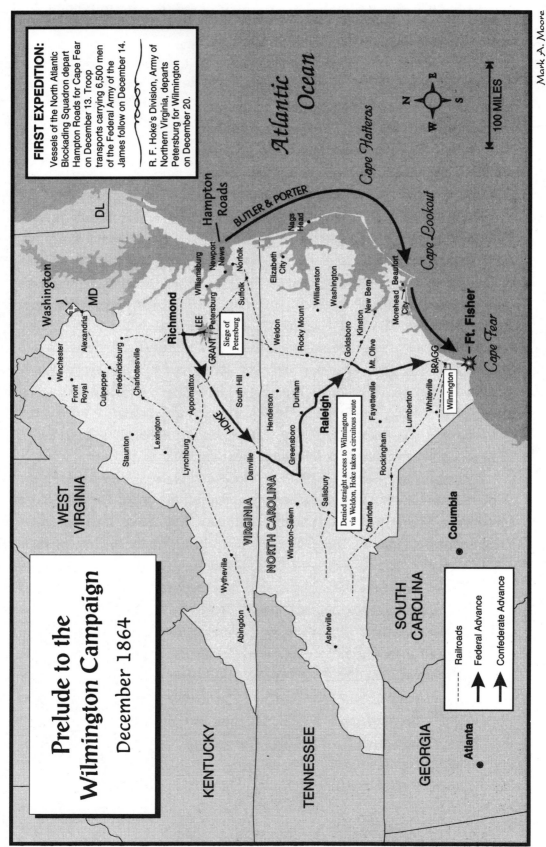

Prelude to the
Wilmington Campaign
December 1864

FIRST EXPEDITION:

Vessels of the North Atlantic Blockading Squadron depart Hampton Roads for Cape Fear on December 13. Troop transports carrying 6,500 men of the Federal Army of the James follow on December 14.

R. F. Hoke's Division, Army of Northern Virginia, departs Petersburg for Wilmington on December 20.

Mark A. Moore

Grant with much confidence for the success of the Fort Fisher mission.

The politics of command was not endemic to the Union, for controversy also haunted the Cape Fear high command. When he was convinced that Wilmington was seriously threatened by attack, President Jefferson Davis replaced the Cape Fear District commander, Maj. Gen. W. H. C. Whiting, with the most controversial and vilified officer in the Confederacy—Gen. Braxton Bragg. Whiting's alleged alcohol abuse had eroded Davis' confidence in the general's ability to defend

Major General Robert Frederick Hoke not only looked like a young Robert E. Lee, but was also considered one of the best commanders in Lee's Army of Northern Virginia. In December 1864, Lee sent Hoke and his 6,400-man division to help defend Wilmington and keep the Confederacy's lifeline open. *U.S. Army Military History Institute*

"Braxton Bragg has been ordered to Wilmington. . . Goodbye Wilmington!"

Wilmington at such a critical hour. Bragg, on the other hand, was the president's friend and trusted advisor, despite the fact that he had resigned in disgrace as commander of the Army of Tennessee after subordinates threatened to munity because of his incompetence following his crushing defeat at Chattanooga in late November 1863. In sending Bragg to take over command at the Cape Fear, the Davis administration, critics howled, was making a big mistake. "Braxton Bragg has been ordered to Wilmington," announced the *Richmond Enquirer.* "Goodbye Wilmington."

Ironically, Bragg's contentious appointment coincided with Lee's distressful warning that if Wilmington fell, he "could not maintain his army." The commanding officer's message was clear. The Confederacy's lifeline through the

city must remain open. The survival of the Army of Northern Virginia depended on it. To help defend the important Carolina seaport, Lee dispatched one of his elite divisions—6,400 troops led by Maj. Gen. Robert F. Hoke—from the lines near Petersburg on December 21. As the Confederate reinforcements travelled southward by rail toward Wilmington, the Union naval task force and army transports made its first appearance off Fort Fisher.

A novel feature of the Federal effort to destroy Fort Fisher was a powder ship. Convinced that a huge army bomb could blow down the sand walls of the mighty stronghold before the navy fired a shot, General Butler had 430,000 pounds of gunpowder loaded into a converted gunboat, the *Louisiana,* with plans to detonate her close by the fort. Such an experiment had not been attempted in the war, but Butler was certain that its success would revolutionize warfare against harbor defenses, for which he could then claim credit. Admiral Porter tried to steal Butler's thunder, however, by exploding the *Louisiana* before the army commander was on the scene. When the powder vessel turned out to be a dud, Porter blamed Butler. Then, determined to take Fort Fisher the old fashioned way, Porter unleashed a two-day bombardment on the fort that was unprecedented in its severity. Porter's warships fired more than 20,000 shot and shell into the sand bastion on December 24-25. Nevertheless, the stout defenses and beleaguered Confederate garrison held their own.

When he finally reached Federal Point, Butler shoveled only a third of his infantry ashore to assault Fort Fisher. General Weitzel advanced with a reconnaissance force, but soon reported from the front that Porter's naval bombardment, despite its intensity, had not damaged the works or its armament enough to justify a ground assault. Already angry over Porter's handling of his pet powder ship project, Butler decided to abort the mission, withdraw his troops, and sail back to Virginia.[4]

The failed expedition sparked a firestorm of controversy in the North which led to Butler's removal from departmental command and a Congressional investigation as to why the combined operation failed. While the politicians huffed and puffed, General Grant turned a serious eye toward capturing Wilmington. Although he had been indifferent to the first expedition, the commanding general's interest was now high. Fortunately for the Union, the defeat at Fort Fisher was partially offset by a concurrent victory when Maj. Gen. William T. Sherman captured Savannah on December 21, 1864.

After his occupation of Atlanta, Sherman led a 60,000-man force virtually unopposed across Georgia and into Savannah. Sherman presented the city as a Christmas gift to President Lincoln. For his part, Grant was relieved to see Sherman safe on the coast and anxious to transfer his powerful legion by sea to Virginia to help drive Lee out of his entrenchments along the Petersburg-Richmond front. But Sherman had other plans. He proposed instead to march his army to Virginia by way of the Carolinas, destroying supply depots and railroads along the way. If need be, he could attack Wilmington from the rear. At any rate, Sherman believed that his advance would force Lee to abandon his entrenched position and move into the open, where Grant and Sherman stood a better chance of defeating him.

Sherman's plan and his confidence in it pleased Grant. The crowning benefit could well be the end of the Confederacy. At the very least, the commanding general believed that a successful campaign would keep the South and its armies in disarray. Grant wrote to Sherman on December 27, authorizing him to begin his "Northern expedition" as soon as possible.

Having agreed to Sherman's bold Carolinas Campaign, Grant was determined to guarantee its success by furnishing "Cump" Sherman's army with reinforcements, supplies, and a haven on the seacoast halfway between Savannah and Petersburg in case Sherman needed to retreat to safety. Wilmington suddenly took on a whole new meaning for Grant: possession of the Cape Fear River and the city's three railroads would best allow him to assist Sherman's army. The transportation routes could be used to funnel soldiers and supplies to Sherman once he reached North Carolina. The irony of sending Union troops and provisions to the front through the same Wilmington pipeline which the Confederates had exploited for years must have crossed Grant's mind. Grant, then, sighted Wilmington in his crosshairs.

To cooperate with the mercurial Admiral Porter, Grant assigned the affable and capable Bvt. Maj. Gen. Alfred Howe Terry, the respected commander of the newly formed XXIV Army Corps in the Army of the James, to command the Wilmington expeditionary force. Despite his renown in the wartime army, Terry is perhaps better known as the commander of the Department of the Dakota at the time of Lt. Col. George Armstrong Custer's defeat and death at the Battle of Little Big Horn in June 1876. Terry's Provisional Corps, as it was officially designated, comprised the same hand-picked troops from Butler's ill-fated attack: Brig. Gen. Adelbert Ames' Second Division, XXIV Army Corps, and two brigades of U.S. Colored Troops, XXV Army Corps, commanded by Brig. Gen. Charles J. Paine. Terry also took along his old Second Brigade, First Division, XXIV Corps. Together with artillery and support personnel, the increased force numbered about 9,600 officers and men.[5]

Porter's warships and Terry's transports reached Fort Fisher during the night of January 12, and opened the battle early the next morning. The navy bombarded the fort for two-and-a-half days, firing almost as many projectiles as in the Christmas attack. While the gunboats pummeled the bastion, General Terry's infantry landed on Federal Point virtually unopposed and advanced toward the fort. Late on the afternoon of January 15, Union ground forces consisting of Adelbert Ames' division and a 2,200-man naval shore party, stormed Fisher.

The Confederate defenders, led by Col. William Lamb and General Whiting, rushed from their underground bombproofs to stave off the assault. They succeeded in quickly turning back the poorly-armed and disorganized naval column, but soon became locked in hand-to-hand combat with Ames' troops, who had secured a lodgment on the fort's land face. The savage, close-quarter fighting raged for more than five hours before the heavily outnumbered and exhausted Southerners were driven from the fort and compelled to surrender. Both Lamb and Whiting were seriously wounded and captured, along with most of their men.

The battle's outcome might have been different had General Braxton Bragg sent in substantial reinforcements from Robert F. Hoke's 6,400-man division, entrenched at Sugar Loaf hill four-and-a-half miles north of Fort Fisher. When he finally responded to Lamb's and Whiting's frantic appeals for outside assistance, Bragg made only a half-hearted attempt to send troops into Fort Fisher by way of the Cape Fear River. Only 350 soldiers of Johnson Hagood's South Carolina Brigade got ashore the morning of the land battle before the troop transport was driven off by the heavy fire of the Union gunboats. Bragg did not make any other attempt to support the defense of the city's key fortification, either by dispatching reinforcements or attacking the Federals. Instead, the man Jefferson Davis had personally sent to save Wilmington kept General Hoke's men sitting on their rifle-muskets at Sugar Loaf, maintaining a position between the enemy and the city. After receiving news of Fisher's fall, President Davis encouraged Bragg to launch a counterattack in an attempt to regain possession of the fort. Bragg refused, fearful that Porter's warships alone would be sufficient to destroy his assaulting force before it could reach the fort. Bragg's abandonment of Fort Fisher raised cries of protest from soldiers and civilians alike, and further eroded his already bad reputation.

Having sacrificed Fisher to save Wilmington, Bragg had little choice but to evacuate the fortifications at Old Inlet and Smithville and withdraw the garrison troops to the new northern defensive line anchored at Fort Anderson on the west bank of the Cape Fear River and Sugar Loaf on the east side. Shocked by the loss of Fort Fisher, despondent Tarheel soldiers abandoned Fort Holmes on Bald Head Island on January 16, and Fort Caswell and its auxillary works on

Brigadier General Louis Hébert commanded at Fort Anderson for ten days in late January 1865, before being replaced because of improprieties. *U.S. Army Military History Institute*

Oak Island the following day. The departing soldiers burned warehouses and barracks and blew up magazines, demolishing part of Fort Caswell in the process. Together with the garri-

"We are now at Fort Anderson and are going to make a stand."

son from Fort Pender at Smithville, the troops retreated to Fort Anderson, where they joined the small garrison force and Hagood's Brigade.[6]

Brigadier General Louis Hébert assumed command of Fort Anderson on January 17, 1865. A Louisiana sugar planter, engineer, and former classmate of Whiting's at West Point, Hébert had served with credit as commander of the fortifications guarding the Cape Fear River inlets in 1864-1865. Hébert's evacuation of those defenses, however, met with derision from some of his soldiers. They believed the withdrawal was disorganized, entailed unnecessary loss of supplies, and was conducted under the auspices of a drunk commander. The latter accusation soon prompted an army investigation, but for the time being Hébert remained in command. "We are now here at Fort Anderson, what is left of us, and it is said are going to make a stand here," wrote Capt. William Henry Tripp of Company B, 40th North Carolina, to his wife, after the regiment had evacuated Bald Head Island. The Cape Fear high command confirmed that belief among the soldiers when it notified Hébert on January 20 that, "unless. . . the necessity is immediate to save your command, you will not give up your present position. . . ."[7]

Hébert feared those orders might soon be put to the test, for the Federals quickly advanced close to Fort Anderson. Within days after their victory at Fort Fisher and the Confederate abandonment of the lower forts, the Federals gained control of the Cape Fear estuary. By the afternoon of January 16, the U.S. Navy gunboats *Tacony* and *Sassacus* had shoved their way through shallow New Inlet and turned their bows upriver. Others vessels soon followed. On January 18, Federal sailors, led by Lt. Cmdr. William B. Cushing, secured possession of the deserted Southern fortifications on Oak Island before proceeding across the harbor to accept the civilian surrender of Smithville. The next day, tars from the *Wilderness* and the *Pequot* captured Fort Holmes and eighteen Confederate stragglers left behind during the hasty withdrawal from Bald Head Island. Sailors also succeeded in capturing several unsuspecting Wilmington-bound blockade runners that were unaware of the port's closure.

By January 19, Union troops occupied the lower end of Federal Point, Bald Head Island, Oak Island and Smithville, while Union warships controlled the river as far north as Battery Lamb on Reeves Point, just four miles below Fort Anderson. Protected by their river gunboats, blue-clad sailors went ashore with impunity at Reeves Point to pillage and burn Battery Lamb, while U.S. Army patrols out of Smithville scouted the Brunswick County roads leading toward Fort Anderson.[8]

Concerned about the marauding enemy and reconnoitering parties, General Hébert requested a squad of horsemen to protect his vulnerable west flank beyond Orton Pond and to patrol the roads near Fort Anderson. Responding to Hébert's call, a small contingent of the 2nd South Carolina Cavalry soon reported, along with instructions from the military authorities for the mounted soldiers to push forward as close to the Union lines as possible, to capture any and all enemy scouts they came upon, and to reconnoiter the Union gunboats entering the river. The cavalrymen were also to prevent slaves from escaping to the Federals. The increasing Union activity in the area could only mean an advance upon Wilmington was imminent. "We have been expecting the Yankees to attack us by land and water but they have not done so thus far," wrote one Confederate officer at Fort Anderson. General Bragg was not optimistic that his defenses, including those at Brunswick Point, could stop a determined enemy assault. "The armament [at Fort Anderson] is not capable of a successful resistance to the enemy's heavy metal," Bragg wrote to Robert E. Lee on January 27. "Should a determined move be made on us by the river, there will be no alternative but to fall back."

Bragg's pessimism did not bode well for Wilmington's survival.[9]

Contrary to Braxton Bragg's fatalistic forecast, the Union army commander was extremely confident of taking Wilmington. Pumped up and excited by his corps' success at Fort Fisher, General Terry was anxious to push upriver. Admiral Porter, however, cautioned against a premature strike on the city. Although he respected the general's audacity, Porter thought it best to wait until reinforcements arrived and his gunboats were resupplied with ammunition. Besides, the labor and stress associated with the Battle of Fort Fisher—the largest combined operation of the war—had taken their toll on the veteran seaman, who desired a much-needed rest before engaging in another hard fight. Porter retired to the cabin of his flagship *Malvern* for a few days, while Terry dug-in and waited for orders to advance.[10]

For a time, conditions were unfavorable for campaigning anyway. Blustery winds, freezing temperatures and incessant rains in late January and early February 1865 made life

Pvt. James Dallas Croom and his first cousin, Pvt. Nathaniel Richardson Croom, Jr. from Colvins' Creek in New Hanover County (present day Pender County), served together in Company B, 1st Battalion North Carolina Heavy Artillery at Fort Anderson in January and February 1865. *Courtesy of James McCallum*

Previously unpublished image of Pvt. Nathaniel Richardson Croom, Jr., Company B, 1st Battalion, North Carolina Heavy Artillery. *Courtesy of Penn Croom*

almost unbearable for Confederate and Union forces in the Lower Cape Fear. Although there were intermittent pleasant days, overall the region's weather was unusually bad. "Oh! it is bitter cold and has been for several days," observed Capt. William Henry Tripp on January 27. Tripp had lost all of his jackets except his overcoat during the evacuation of Fort Holmes, and it offered little protection from the cold by the time he reached Fort Anderson. Nevertheless, the captain fared better than many of his soldiers of Company B, 40th North Carolina Regiment, who, Tripp claimed, were "without shoes almost entirely."

Wilmington-born Lt. William Calder, adjutant of the 1st Battalion North Carolina Heavy Artillery, echoed Tripp's assessment of the bad weather. "I think it is as cold weather as I ever felt," Calder wrote to his mother from Fort Anderson. The young lieutenant awoke one evening soaked to the skin by a chilly rain and resulting pools of water which had formed

under him. "Tried to lay there & sleep it out but couldn't do it," the young officer recorded in his diary. "Got up and built a large fire around which we stood until morning, altogether a miserable night." According to Calder, rain fell "without intermission" the first three or four days of his stay at Fort Anderson, from January 19-23.[11]

For Confederate soldiers used to garrison life, camping in the woods and trenches at Fort Anderson was rough going. The fort's barracks, built early in the war, were too few in number and too small to quarter the more than 2,000 troops suddenly thrown together. Even for those soldiers fortunate enough to find space in the barracks, accomodations were tight. Captain Tripp and four other men stayed in a "little house" Tripp described as being about the size of his wife's garden shed. "Three of us sleep on a bunk and the other two sleep on the floor under the bunk," the captain explained. "Close stowing I assure you."[12]

The lack of sufficient housing at Fort Anderson forced the vast majority of both the enlisted men and officers to "sleep along the line of breastworks in whatever rude shelters they [could] construct." William Calder and his bunkmates—Lt. Col. John Douglas Taylor of the 36th North Carolina Regiment and Maj. Alexander MacRae of the 1st Battalion North Carolina Heavy Artillery—built a shanty of planks, logs, and sand over a thick pile of pine straw near the earthworks. Captain William Badham, Jr., commander of Company B, 3rd Battalion North Carolina Light Artillery, and two of his friends erected a lean-to of pine poles and planks in back of the trenches and kept a fire burning at the shelter's opening. "When the rain comes from behind we fare very well— when in front, terribly," Badham observed. While providing the soldiers with much needed shelter and fuel, the felled trees from around the fort also exposed the men to cold winds "sharp enough to cut a man in two," exclaimed one soldier. "This life goes rather hard with these men who have been living in forts since the commencement of the war," William Calder remarked.[13]

"This life goes rather hard with these men who have been living in forts."

To make matters worse, rations were in short supply at Fort Anderson since the river above was closed to most traffic because of the growing threat of Union warships just downstream. "[We eat a lot of] corn bread," declared one Confederate officer. As their hunger grew, the soldiers took to hunting deer, rabbits, wild turkeys and even cattle and sheep in the woods surrounding the fort. They also foraged for pigs, chickens and goats on farms and plantations some distance away. "We are living quite hard here as the supply of provisions is nearly run out," lamented Captain Tripp in early February. "We have beef and mutton and you know that is not good out of the woods at this time of year." Lieutenant Zaccheus Ellis of Company B, 1st Battalion North Carolina Heavy Artillery, recorded that he and his comrades were "faring only tolerably [at Fort Anderson]. All the meat we get we have to hunt in the woods. We kill and eat everything from an old cow down to a yearling," he continued. "It looks like a waste of property to kill such poor and small cattle, but we received orders that our dependence for forage and meat was in Brunswick County so we had to begin the impressing business."[14]

Victims of the "impressing business" by both Confederate and Federal troops defined the practice as merciless confiscation, if not downright theft. Civilian complaints of depredations, especially among Hagood's South Carolina soldiers, became so commonplace that General

Bragg asked Robert F. Hoke, headquartered at Sugar Loaf, to personally visit Fort Anderson to investigate. When General Hoke was unable to make the trip across the river because of ill health, Bragg dispatched an assistant inspector general, Lt. Col. George T. Gordon, to check out the "numerous reports of drunkenness, straggling, plundering, and demoralization of every sort." Even General Hébert was "represented as being himself compromised." Gordon's report apparently cast grave doubts about Hébert's sobriety, and thus his reliabilty, for the general was quickly transferred out of the district and assigned an administrative position as chief engineer with the Department of North Carolina.[15]

A drunk and irresponsible commander, poor living conditions, lack of food, bad weather, and the continued presence of strong enemy forces all had a detrimental effect on soldiers at Fort Anderson. Illness swept through the ranks.

"My men are getting quite sickly here, some with one thing and others with another," reported Tripp. Bad colds seemed to have been the most common malady among the men, but Pvt. Aaron Cox of Captain Tripp's company became so sick that he was transferred from Fort Anderson on January 24 to a hospital in Wilmington for treatment. On the same day, one of Cox's comrades, Pvt. William T. Holsomback, was granted a sixty-day furlough home to recover from an illness. Private Isaiah Smithwick, also of Company B, 40th North Carolina, died of pneumonia at Fort Anderson on the night of February 6. The rampant sickess caused morale in the ranks to plummet. Distraught by the state of affairs at Fort Anderson, some boys simply ran away. "There has been a great deal of desertions from our troop since Ft Fisher fell," admitted one Southern officer. "Hardly a day or night passes but some two or more leaves [and] there has gone off as high as 25 in one night." While most soldiers remained in Fort Anderson's trenches and stayed loyal to the Confederate cause, the high command grew more concerned about desertion. General Bragg hoped that a change in commanders at Anderson would solve that and other problems.[16]

With Hébert's departure, command of Fort Anderson was assigned to Brig. Gen. Johnson Hagood. The general's South Carolina troops were already at the Brunswick bastion, having been sent there after the feeble attempt to reinforce Fort Fisher with them on January 15. When Hagood returned to the Cape Fear on January 27 from a furlough in his home state, he was immediately sent to Fort Anderson to take charge. "Genl Hébert has just been removed from the command of our Brigade and we are now under the command of Genl Hagood," wrote a Confederate officer to his wife. "General Hagood is said to be a nice man and a good officer." Hagood was also considered a strict disciplinarian who, General Bragg hoped, would redress the bad behavior of his own men.[17]

Hagood's association with the military went back to his early youth. Born in Barnwell County, South Carolina, in 1829, Hagood entered the South Carolina Military Academy (now the Citadel) at age fourteen. After graduating in 1847, he practiced law, planted cotton, and paraded with the state militia. When the Civil War broke out, Hagood set aside his practice and plow to command the 1st South Carolina Infantry at the attack on Fort Sumter. With the exception of his brief appearance at First Manassas in Virginia in mid-July 1861, Hagood spent most of the war commanding South Carolina troops on the Sea Islands defending Charleston. When the famed 54th Massachusetts Colored Infantry charged Battery Wagner in July 1863, Hagood was in overall command of the Morris Island defenders who repulsed the attack. Hagood commanded on James Island until his transfer to Virginia with his superior, Gen. P. G. T. Beauregard, who was summoned to defend Petersburg in the spring of 1864.

Hagood led his brigade in actions at Bermuda Hundred, Drewry's Bluff, Cold Harbor and the Weldon Railroad. During the autumn of 1864, Hagood's South Carolina troops endured hard duty in the trenches around Petersburg before traveling south with Hoke's Division to defend Wilmington. After the Fort Fisher debacle, survivors of Hagood's Brigade were withdrawn to Fort Anderson. Although he was considered by many people who met him to be haughty, somber, and aloof, Johnson Hagood was respected by his Palmetto State comrades.[18]

By the time Hagood assumed command at Anderson in late January, his own brigade had dwindled to 926 enlisted men and 63 officers. It was comprised of the 7th South Carolina Battalion, the 11th South Carolina Infantry, remnants of the 21st and 25th South Carolina Infantry regiments, and the 27th South Carolina Infantry. The 21st and 25th regiments had been especially hard hit by casualties during Second Fort Fisher. Standing alongside the Palmetto State infantry were about 1,100 Tarheel soldiers and officers under the overall command of Col. John J. Hedrick, 40th North Carolina Regiment (3rd North Carolina Artillery), who was one-time head of Fort Anderson. Lumped together as Hedrick's Brigade were four companies of the 1st Battalion North Carolina Heavy Artillery, gunners of the 36th North Carolina Regiment who had escaped the Fort Fisher fight, and six companies of artillerymen of the 40th North Carolina Regiment. Captain Abner A. Moseley's Sampson Artillery; Capt. William Badham, Jr's Company B, 3rd Battalion North Carolina Light Artillery; teenaged boys of Company B, 2nd North Carolina Junior Reserves; Capt. W. J. McDougald's Unattached Company of North Carolina Troops; a detached unit of Coast Guard; and a contingent of 152 riders of the 2nd South Carolina Cavalry, together with various support personnel, rounded out

Haughty, somber but respected, South Carolina Brig. Gen. Johnson Hagood was assigned to command at Fort Anderson in late January 1865, and led its defense against a Union juggernaut three weeks later. *U.S. Army Military History Institute*

Hagood's force of about 2,300 effectives. And Fort Anderson is where they would make their stand against the Federals. Reiterating an earlier memorandum on the fort's importance to Wilmington's safety, the Cape Fear high command informed General Hagood on February 8, that, "except in an extreme case, involving the safety of the command, the present position would not be abandoned."[19]

From a military point of view, Wilmington still retained some importance even after its closure as a blockade running seaport. Bragg's force distracted the attention of a sizeable Union corps that would otherwise be battling Lee in Virginia. While Lee could ill-afford to leave Hoke's division at the Cape Fear, its detachment, nonetheless, might prove beneficial. Wilmington needed to be safeguarded at least until government stores and property could be removed. More importantly, the Richmond authorities instructed Bragg to do everything in his power to keep the Federals in check at the Cape Fear, thereby preventing Terry's Provisional Corps from reinforcing General Sherman. As a result, it was imperative that Hoke hold Sugar Loaf and Hagood hold

Fort Anderson. "We will resist every advance, and trust in God to give us the victory," boasted Lt. William Calder, stationed at Fort Anderson. "I trust He may enable us to save our homes from the enemy."[20]

General U. S. Grant also trusted in God to grant the Union a victory at Wilmington. By late January 1865, the commanding officer was so intent on capturing Wilmington that he left the Virginia battlefront—a rare move for him—to travel to the Cape Fear to confer with Admiral Porter and General Terry about capturing the city. Accompanying Grant were Assistant Secretary of the Navy Gustavus V. Fox and Maj. Gen. John McAllister Schofield, commander of the XXIII Corps, Army of the Ohio. For three-and-a-half hours on the night of January 28, the commanders studied maps and charts on board Porter's flagship on the Cape Fear River. Grant was determined to hammer out a strategy to open the railways between the seacoast and Goldsboro, North Carolina, in order to meet

The Cape Fear River squadron flagship *U.S.S. Malvern,* on board which Admiral Porter hosted a council of war for Generals U.S. Grant, John M. Schofield, and Alfred H. Terry and Asst. Sec. of the Navy Gustavus V. Fox, on the night of January 28, 1865. *U.S. Army Military History Institute*

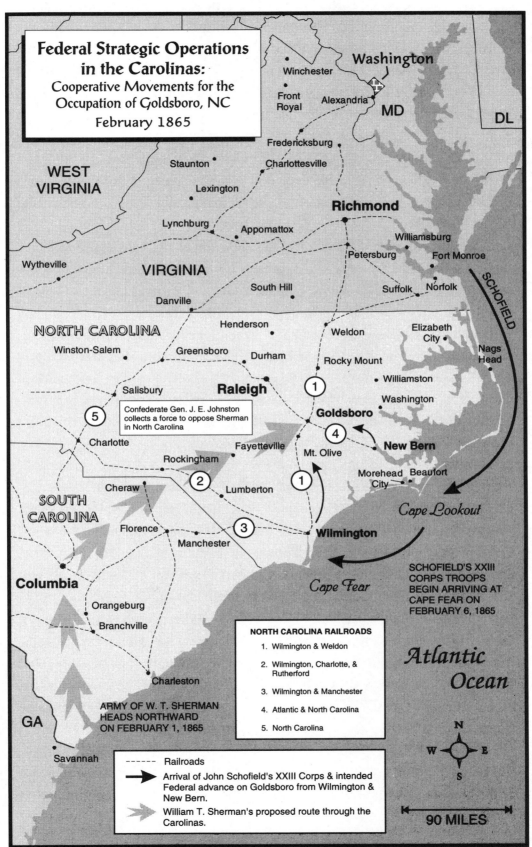

Federal Strategic Operations in the Carolinas:
Cooperative Movements for the Occupation of Goldsboro, NC
February 1865

Confederate Gen. J. E. Johnston collects a force to oppose Sherman in North Carolina

SCHOFIELD'S XXIII CORPS TROOPS BEGIN ARRIVING AT CAPE FEAR ON FEBRUARY 6, 1865

NORTH CAROLINA RAILROADS

1. Wilmington & Weldon
2. Wilmington, Charlotte, & Rutherford
3. Wilmington & Manchester
4. Atlantic & North Carolina
5. North Carolina

ARMY OF W. T. SHERMAN HEADS NORTHWARD ON FEBRUARY 1, 1865

------ Railroads

→ Arrival of John Schofield's XXIII Corps & intended Federal advance on Goldsboro from Wilmington & New Bern.

⇒ William T. Sherman's proposed route through the Carolinas.

90 MILES

Atlantic Ocean

Mark A. Moore

Sherman with reinforcements and supplies for his army.[21]

Sherman, for his part, was ready to invade the Carolinas, targeting Columbia, South Carolina first, and then Fayetteville, North Carolina, both of which housed Confederate armories. Sherman's ultimate object, however, was Goldsboro, North Carolina, whose capture would be advantageous for two reasons. First, Goldsboro was the junction for two coastal railroads—the Wilmington & Weldon and the Atlantic & North Carolina to New Bern—by which Sherman could be resupplied and reinforced. Second, from Goldsboro Sherman could easily strike the state capital of Raleigh, where Confederate supplies from Wilmington were being sent. "If Lee lets us get [Goldsboro], he is gone up," Sherman predicted. "[From there] I can easily take Raleigh, when it seems that Lee must come out of his trenches or allow his army to be absolutely invested." With Fort Fisher in Union hands, Sherman saw little reason to attack Wilmington, whose fall, he believed, was now inevitable.[22]

At their Cape Fear meeting, Grant agreed with the advice of his subordinates that Wilmington was the best point from which to move toward Goldsboro with a support force for Sherman. Although New Bern possessed a deeper harbor more favorable for a supply base, the railroad from there to Goldsboro needed extensive repairs. Grant assumed that the presence of Bragg's army at Wilmington was an indication that the city's railroads were still operational. A bold strike might capture the rail lines and rolling stock before the Confederates could destroy or remove them. While the Union possession of Fort Fisher gave Sherman a safe haven on the seaboard, he might need Wilmington as a supply depot and as a place to concentrate troops south of Goldsboro. Grant, therefore, deemed "the capture of Wilmington of the greatest importance."[23]

Having studied the defenses protecting Wilmington's approaches, Porter and Terry recommended advancing against the city by way of Fort Anderson on the west side of the Cape Fear River. "There is only one important work between us and Wilmington—Fort Anderson, which is very strong, and the army also has heavy lines of earthworks in its front," Porter explained. "We will be bothered in the river with the obstructions, which are of no ordinary kind." Even if Anderson's water obstructions stymied the navy's efforts, the mainland would provide the army with more space to maneuver than was available on the narrow Federal Point peninsula. Porter's and Terry's plan of attack was straightforward. While the navy bombarded Fort Anderson, the army would launch a frontal ground assault against the fort or attempt to outflank it by going around Orton Pond. As was the case at Fort Fisher, cooperation between the U.S. Navy and Army would be the key to a successful undertaking against the Brunswick stronghold. Grant approved the maneuver, stating emphatically, "it is the best and only thing to be done."[24]

According to Porter, the operation would require at least 13,000 troops, about 4,000 more than Terry commanded on Federal Point. Grant, however, had already provided for such a contingency by ordering John M. Schofield's 21,000-man XXIII Army Corps from Tennessee to support Terry's efforts to take Fort Fisher and Wilmington—or to reinforce Sherman's army in Georgia. Grant concluded that there was greater need for the XXIII Corps in the proposed move against Wilmington, and he instructed Schofield to transfer his force to the Lower Cape Fear as soon as possible. Upon his return to Virginia, Grant asked the War Department to assign Schofield commander of the Department of North Carolina.[25]

Despite Schofield's inexperience in combined operations, Grant considered the appointment a good one. Schofield was a West Point graduate,

The appointment of Maj. Gen. John McAllister Schofield, commander of the XXIII Army Corps, to head Union military operations against Fort Anderson and Wilmington aroused the indignation of other leaders, but Schofield proved to be a capable leader. *Author's Collection*

a regular army officer and a reasonably successful and dependable corps commander. Early in the war, Schofield had served as departmental commander in both Missouri and Arkansas. During Sherman's Atlanta campaign in the summer of 1864, Schofield led the Army of the Ohio (XXIII Corps). After the fall of Atlanta in September, Sherman turned east and marched to the sea, leaving Schofield behind with Maj. Gen. George H. Thomas to oppose General John Bell Hood's Army of Tennessee. Schofield's corps crippled Hood's attacking army at Franklin on November 30, 1864, a defensive victory that contributed greatly to Thomas' crushing defeat of Hood's remaining force at Nashville two weeks later.

Chubby, almost boyish in appearance despite his balding head and scraggly reddish beard, Schofield proved an intensely ambitious man. Despite being perceived by fellow officers as somewhat petty, Schofield also enjoyed a stellar reputation as an able organizer and administrator. Overall, he was a sound choice for the Department of North Carolina command.[26]

Grant's command reorganization disappointed Admiral Porter and General Terry, both of whom were confident that with Schofield's reinforcements they could capture Fort Anderson and Wilmington themselves. For his part, Grant paid little heed or was oblivious to the controversy Schofield's appointment aroused. His only concern was capturing the "city by the sea." The lieutenant general instructed Schofield to advance on Wilmington by way of Fort Anderson, and then to move rapidly toward Goldsboro. Schofield's objectives were to provide Sherman with supplies and manpower, as needed, open a base of supply for Sherman's army at or near Goldsboro, and prevent Braxton Bragg from impeding Sherman's advance. Grant believed that once Sherman and Schofield joined forces, the Confederates would be unable to muster an army in North Carolina strong enough to threaten them. As a result, Lee's rear would be vulnerable to an attack.[27]

Sherman advanced northward from Savannah on February 1, 1865, while Schofield prepared to embark on the Wilmington Campaign. After a brief delay due to cold weather, Schofield and the XXIII Corps' Third Division, Maj. Gen. Jacob Dolson Cox commanding, set sail on February 4 from Alexandria, Virginia. The remainder of the corps shipped out in the following two weeks as transports became available and the weather permitted.[28]

Admiral Porter and General Terry wasted little time awaiting Schofield's arrival, but prepared instead to move on Wilmington. Terry's soldiers continued to reconnoiter Confederate defenses on Federal Point, probing for weak spots along the lines, while Porter assembled a flotilla of some thirty vessels on the Cape Fear River for the attack on Fort Anderson. Porter's impressive force comprised mostly side-wheel gunboats capable of operating in the river's narrow and shallow channel. "The Channel is very narrow and runs very near the Fort, but few ships can operate at a time," observed one Union naval officer on board the *Lenapee*. The *Lenapee* and other so called double-enders like her—the *Maratanza* and *Mackinaw* among them—were designed to sail frontward or backward with a rudder at both ends.[29]

The flotilla of double-enders was supplemented by the *Montauk*, a light draft monitor sent from the Charleston blockading squadron specifically for operations on the shallow Cape Fear River. As the third monitor commissioned by the U.S. Navy on December 17, 1862, the *Montauk* was immediately sent south to take part in the naval attack on Fort McAllister

guarding Savannah, Georgia in late January 1863. The following month she was damaged by a torpedo during a fight with the Confederate steamer *Nashville*. After undergoing repairs, the single turreted ironclad spent the next two years engaging various forts and batteries around Charleston, before being dispatched to the Lower Cape Fear, where she arrived on or about January 24, 1865.

Despite her impressive wartime record, the *Montauk* is perhaps best known for her association with President Abraham Lincoln's tragic death. On her deck the body of the president's assassin, John Wilkes Booth, was autopsied on April 27, 1865. Most of Booth's co-conspirators were imprisoned on the floating fortress before their trial and execution. Ironically, a cheerful Abraham Lincoln had visited with sailors on board the *Montauk* at Washington's Navy Yard late on the afternoon of April 14, just hours before he was struck down by his enraged killer at Ford's Theater. Two months before that fateful day, the *Montauk* played a key role in Union naval operations against Fort Anderson.[30]

Captain Abner A. Moseley's Sampson Artillery fired its 12-pounder Whitworth cannon from behind these emplacements constructed adjacent to Battery B at Fort Anderson. The Cape Fear River is behind the trees in the background. *Author's Collection*

Bolstered by the addition of the *Montauk*, the U.S. Navy's Cape Fear River squadron spent much of late January and early February 1865 preparing to attack Fort Anderson. While sailors readied their cannon and stockpiled ammunition, Admiral Porter sent gunboats upriver to take soundings and make onshore observations. "We can plainly see the Rebs at work upon [Fort Anderson]," noted one Union sailor. Operating just offshore, the gunboats could not resist the temptation of firing a shell or two at Anderson's defenders, who were preparing their works for the impending battle. The harassing fire sometimes provoked the Confederates to reply in kind. "We occasionally send a 100 lb shell directly into the Ft.," noted a Union tar on board the *Lenapee*. "In return they open upon us with their long range Whitworth guns sending shot and shell beyond us and some of them come very near us."[31]

The defiant exchanges between the Union gunboats and Fort Anderson occurred off and on during the mid-winter weeks. At two o'clock on the afternoon of January 22, Lt. Cmdr. Daniel L. Braine's *Pequot* ascended the river and fired seven 100-pounder Parrott shells in an attempt to draw the fire of Fort Anderson and learn the precise number of cannon mounted in the fort. One Parrott shell struck a warehouse along the riverfront, but otherwise the *Pequot*'s shots caused little dam-

Previously unpublished wartime image of Capt. William Henry Tripp, who lost six men of Company B, 40th North Carolina Regiment, by the explosion of a single shell fired from the *U.S.S. Tacony* on Fort Anderson on February 3, 1865. *Courtesy of Tom Morgan*

age. The Southerners replied with their light artillery—six shots from a 12-pounder Whitworth gun—but declined to reveal their big guns. After remaining in range for about two hours, a frustrated Commander Braine withdrew the *Pequot* to her anchorage downstream. Braine later reported that he had counted six smoothbore cannon in the fort. Another Union sailor concluded that the Confederates' reluctance to use their heavy cannon on the gunboats "in easy range," showed their desire "to be let alone and prepare themselves for a general engagement." About mid-afternoon on January 30, the monitor *Montauk* fired several shots at Fort Anderson, but the cannonballs did little more than make the Confederates duck their heads.[32]

While the U.S. Navy did not provoke a general engagement, it found itself in a tough scrap with Fort Anderson on February 3. The *Tacony*, one of the first gunboats to enter the Cape Fear River after the fall of Fort Fisher, steamed upriver and at 3:55 p.m. began firing on the Brunswick fort. Her second shot proved to be the most destructive, tearing into a barrack and wounding six men.[33]

The incoming shell startled soldiers of Company B, 40th North Carolina Regiment lounging inside their quarters. When the projectile burst upon impact, Pvt. Alfred Robason was "torn up" by flying shrapnel. The wound proved mortal, and Robason died two days later.

Chunks of hot whizzing iron also fractured Pvt. Robert Greene's skull and ripped the flesh from Pvt. Bracey E. Jackson's face and one of his arms. Although Sgt. John A. Thomas and Pvt. John L. Potter escaped with only slight wounds, Pvt. William Whitaker was wounded "right bad"

The U.S. Navy...found itself in a tough scrap with Fort Anderson on February 3.

in the leg. The injured soldiers' commanding officer, Capt. William Henry Tripp, also came close to getting hurt by the "metallic coffin." Standing just outside the barrack, Captain Tripp was covered with dirt thrown up by the exploding projectile. As the only officer to lose men during the bombardment, Tripp was angry that his soldiers had not followed orders, thereby heedlessly exposing themselves. "Had my men done as they were directed none would have got hurt," Tripp maintained. "They will look out hereafter."[34]

As Captain Tripp rushed to the aid of his wounded troops, others planned their retaliation. Captain Abner A. Moseley's Sampson Artillery fired at least five shots from its 12-pounder Whitworth rifle-cannon. The Whitworth was noted for its deadly accuracy and spiralled projectiles that whistled eerily in flight. Three Whitworth bolts struck the *Tacony*, including one that went through the superstructure and another that penetrated her hull below the waterline, causing a dangerous leak. The damaged vessel beat a hasty retreat downstream to safety. "We gave her some dozen shots before she got out of range, striking her three times, one shot passing completely through her," claimed one of Anderson's defenders. "From the manner in which she got away it is supposed that she will not trouble us again soon."[35]

Despite the Southerners' bravado, the *Shawmut* replaced the *Tacony* on the firing line about 4:50 p.m., unleashing a dozen 30-pounder Parrott shells on the fort. Together, the double-ender gunboats fired only twenty-six rounds, yet they struck with "infernal accuracy,

The *U.S.S. Shawmut* unleashed a dozen 30-pounder Parrott shells on Fort Anderson during the late afternoon of February 3, 1865. Even the Confederate defenders admitted the gunboat fired "some good shots" at them. *U.S. Army Military History Institute*

nearly every shot falling within the work," a Union eyewitness attested. One of Fort Anderson's occupants, however, claimed that with the exception of "some good shots," most of the naval projectiles fell short of their target. Despite the late afternoon attack, the shelling caused no serious damage to the earthworks or its armament.[36]

At least one more brief duel between Union gunboats and Fort Anderson occurred before a serious effort was made to take the fort. Shortly before 6:00 p.m. on February 10, the *Huron* proceeded upriver and opened fire. The Brunswick artillerists answered with four or five shots before the brief engagement ended. The navy bombarded the Confederate stronghold in order to establish its effective range of fire, as well as to annoy the enemy. "One vessel ascends up and opens fire on Fort Anderson, and retires for another, so we continually harass the Rebs, and try to prevent them from building batteries [and] mount guns on the Fort," explained one Union naval officer. "With a glass we can see the Rebs working on Ft Anderson and when they get it done we will try to take it," he boasted. The efficacy of the navy's long arm would prove beneficial in supporting the army's advance on Fort Anderson and Wilmington.[37]

Previously unpublished image of Union Maj. Gen. Jacob Dolson Cox, an Ohio-born volunteer officer who commanded four brigades of the XXIII Army Corps in the Battle of Fort Anderson. *Author's Collection*

The first troops of General Schofield's XXIII Corps slated to attack Fort Anderson began arriving at the Cape Fear on the afternoon of February 6. Ships bearing additional reinforcements straggled in for two days, a gale having slowed their voyage down the treacherous North Carolina coast, which was known by mariners through the centuries as the "Sailors' Grave." Fog, high winds, and heavy seas kept the soldiers of Maj. Gen. Jacob D. Cox's Third Division from going ashore until the morning of February 8, and even then the weather remained bad. General Schofield was one of the first men to hit Federal Point beach. Wasting no time, the Western Theater veteran immediately took command and established his headquarters. General Cox did not land until February 10, setting up his division encampment in rear of General Terry's corps two miles north of Fort Fisher.

Although not a soldier by profession, Jacob Dolson Cox had risen swiftly through the volunteer ranks to become the XXIII Corps' senior division commander. Schofield thought highly enough of Cox's command to bring it with him to the Cape Fear, before transferring his other two divisions. The Canadian-born Cox was a lawyer of considerable renown in Warren, Ohio, during the 1850s. As a devout anti-slavery man, he helped establish the Ohio Republican Party. When the Civil War began, Cox organized and trained Ohio state troops. Within a month he was commissioned a brigadier general in the U.S. Army, and went on to serve with distinction under Maj. Gen. George B. McClellan and Brig. Gen. William S. Rosecrans in the western Virginia Campaign of 1861. Moving east in the summer of 1862, Cox and his Kanawha division fought gallantly as part of the IX Army Corps at South Mountain, the prelude to the Battle of Sharpsburg. Cox spent the following year commanding Union forces in western Virginia and the Department of Ohio, and in the middle of December 1863, assumed command of the newly formed XXIII Army Corps' Third Division. He fought his men with distinction under Schofield in the Atlanta Campaign and in the battles of Franklin and Nashville. In the midst of the Tennessee battles, Cox was confirmed as major general.

Cox's transfer to the Cape Fear marked his first experience in combined operations, although the Ohio general believed his veteran troops would perform as well on the sandy beaches of southeastern North Carolina as they had on the rolling hills of Georgia and Tennessee. His division consisted of three veteran brigades commanded respectively by Cols. Oscar W. Sterl, John S. "Jack" Casement, and Thomas J. Henderson. Once all of Cox's troops were ashore on Federal Point,

When General Braxton Bragg left for Richmond on a military business trip the day before Federal forces launched their attack on Wilmington, most citizens believed the commanding Confederate officer was abandoning the port town to the enemy and getting himself out of harm's way. *U.S. Army Military History Institute*

the transports returned to Alexandria, Virginia, to transfer Schofield's other two divisions.[38]

The massive Union build-up on Federal Point worried Braxton Bragg, who informed North Carolina's Governor Vance that he believed the concentration of enemy troops indicated a movement against Wilmington and Raleigh at an early date. Bragg urged the governor to promptly forward all the troops he could muster for Wilmington's defense. At the same time, the commanding general began quietly removing government and private property of military value from Wilmington, and threatened to destroy remaining cotton, tobacco, naval stores and other commodities that could be of use to the enemy. He also imposed a blackout of military news, refusing to discuss affairs at Fort Anderson and Sugar Loaf. That decision frustrated the families and friends of soldiers stationed at those points, who desperately wanted to hear something more than wild rumors on the streets and the frequent rumbling of heavy cannon fire downriver. Still, Bragg remained silent. "Is it a military necessity to keep our people ignorant of every occurence connected with their interests?" a Wilmingtonian wanted to know. "The stereotyped phraseology of 'all quiet below' will have no effect upon us. We place no confidence in such reports."[39]

The criticism bothered Bragg, but his next move fanned the flames of discontent even higher. As if turning his back on Wilmington's fate, Bragg relinquished his command to Maj. Gen. Robert F. Hoke and left for Richmond on February 10, the eve of the Union drive on Wilmington. From a public relations standpoint, the trip was an ill-timed disaster that only renforced Bragg's reputation for "being not a fighting general." Bragg's explanation for his absence at such a critical hour was that he had been summoned to Virginia by the high command to reorganize his staff.[40]

To most Wilmingtonians, Bragg's reason for leaving seemed more like an excuse to remove himself from harm's way. They viewed Bragg's actions as a clear sign that he planned to abandon Fort Anderson and the city as he had Fort Fisher. As the Federal tempest gathered downstream, citizens lost all remaining trust in his leadership. "General Bragg's presence has been felt as a harbinger of disaster, an omen of impending evil—like a dark, cold, dreary cloud," noted one critic. Lieutenant William Calder observed that the general feeling among Wilmingtonians was a lack of faith in the local Confederate leadership. "The [people] have no confidence in Gen'l Bragg," Calder lamented.[41]

On the same day that Bragg left for Richmond, Schofield, Cox, Terry and Admiral Porter held a council of war on board the *Malvern* to "forge a thunderbolt," as one reporter described it. Time was of the essence, as Sherman's army had been on the march northward from Savannah for ten days. As a result of the conference, Schofield decided to begin active operations without waiting for the remainder of his corps to reach the Cape Fear.

He believed he could capture Fort Anderson and Wilmington with the 13,500 troops he had on hand.[42]

As Schofield and his staff planned the action, Admiral Porter dispatched reconnoitering parties toward Fort Anderson to learn its strength and to search for an enemy ironclad ram rumored to be on the Cape Fear River. The ram was of immediate concern to the chief naval officer, for it could wreck havoc on his unsuspecting ships, particularly after nightfall. Sailors reportedly spotted the iron titan upriver near Orton Point lighthouse on February 5, but its existence could not be confirmed. Porter's anxiety grew when a runaway slave pulled up in a

---

[The Union officers] held a council of war to "forge a thunderbolt..."

---

canoe alongside the *Malvern* one evening to warn the navy of an impending Confederate ram attack. Although suspicious of the slave's story, the admiral still made preparations to receive the enemy craft, deploying two launches from each Union warship onto the river. Each small boat carried well-armed sailors and a heavy net on a pole to disable the enemy ironclad's propeller, which would allow the tars to storm aboard.

Initially, it appeared as if the navy's efforts had bagged the quarry. Shortly after retiring to his cabin late one night, Admiral Porter was startled by loud shouts. The yelling was quickly followed by small arms fire and cheering. As the half-dressed executive officer dashed to the deck of his flagship, the river was alive with small boats rowing furiously toward the scene of the commotion. The yelling and firing continued for several minutes, punctuated by discharges of howitzers and musketry from on board some of the Union gunboats. "That is

Previously unpublished portrait of Lt. Cmdr. William Barker Cushing, whose daring deeds behind enemy lines, dash for adventure and good looks earned him great respect from his fellow U.S. Navy comrades, as well as considerable attention from the ladies. *Author' Collection*

sheer folly," Porter screamed. "They will never capture the thing that way." The admiral shouted instructions for his sailors to pull alongside the ironclad and board her "at all hazards." After more clattering and confusion, a cry arose from the darkness: "we've got him."

Admiral Porter gave a sigh of great relief as Fleet Capt. K. Randolph Breese came aboard the *Malvern* to report on the successful capture.

"Well, sir, we got him," said the captain.

"And a time they had of it," Porter barked. "Why didn't those fellows do as I told them—jam his screw with the nets?"

"He hadn't any screw, sir," replied Breese.

"Then what had he?" Porter retorted.

Captain Breese chuckled: "It was something worse than a ram; it was the biggest bull I ever saw. I don't wonder they took him for a torpedo boat," he remarked.

"A bull!" Porter exclaimed, as he roared with laughter. "And so I am not to see a ram after all." The admiral later wrote that the episode was "so much more ridiculous in reality than in the narration."[43]

The capture of the giant bull notwithstanding, Admiral Porter believed there might yet be a Confederate ironclad on the river waiting for an opportune moment to attack his flotilla. He ordered his sailors to keep a sharp lookout, and on two successive nights he dispatched Lt. Cmdr. William B. Cushing and a hand-picked crew from the *Monticello* to reconnoiter on the Cape Fear River.

Among the many capable officers in David D. Porter's service, none enjoyed the admiral's confidence and trust more than William Barker Cushing. By February 1865, the twenty-two-year-old Cushing was a living legend in the U.S. Navy and his name was well known in most American households. Courageous, bold, and impetuous, he had made several daring raids behind enemy lines attempting to capture blockade runners, kidnap a Confederate general, and sabotage harbor-defending ironclads.

While his efforts rarely succeeded, he never failed to strike fear in the hearts of his antagonists, win their respect, and receive considerable publicity. Cushing was best known for having sunk the Confederate ironclad ram *Albemarle* at Plymouth, North Carolina on October 27, 1864. It was a deed for which he received the Thanks of the U.S. Congress, a promotion to lieutenant commander, and lasting fame. Cushing spent most of his wartime service, however, with the Cape Fear blockading squadron.

During First Fort Fisher, Cushing took soundings off New Inlet while under heavy Confederate artillery fire. In the second battle, Cushing led a group of volunteer sailors from his ship, the *Monticello*, in the navy's ill-fated shore assault. Three days after Fisher's fall, the brash young lieutenant commander accepted the surrender of Smithville from the town's mayor, and then audaciously declared himself governor of the province. During the early morning hours of January 20, Cushing almost single-handedly captured the blockade runner *Charlotte* when her astonished crew dropped anchor at Smithville. No other sailor in Porter's command could match Cushing's dash, daring and zest for excitement and adventure.[44]

As the navy prepared to advance toward Wilmington, Cushing made secret forays into enemy territory. On the afternoon of February 8, he surprised and captured eight Confederate soldiers with rifle-muskets in hand. The next morning, under a flag of truce, Cushing went onshore at Fort Anderson to obtain the personal belongings of his captives, (who were to be shipped north to a prisoner-of-war camp), and to boast, no doubt, of his "recent acquisition" to the dumbfounded garrison.[45]

The following night, February 10, Cushing undertook a more important mission for Admiral Porter—a reconnaissance of the Cape Fear River defenses and to search for the alleged enemy ironclad. Cushing's party

Postwar image of Lt. Col. John Douglas Taylor of the 36th North Carolina Regiment, whose impromptu speech to his soldiers at Fort Anderson on the night of February 11, 1865, was overheard by U.S. Navy commando William B. Cushing, and later reported in the leading New York newspapers. *Courtesy of John Douglas Taylor and Walker Taylor, III*

(including William's brother Milton, a U.S. Navy paymaster) scouted far upstream, viewing obstructions in the river abreast of Fort Anderson and a series of eastern shore batteries three miles below Wilmington. While Cushing claimed to have glimpsed the Confederate gunboat *Chickamauga*, he failed to find the phantom torpedo ram. The famous lieutenant commander tempted capture when, on the trip back downriver, he and his men were forced to lift their small boats over Fort Anderson's jetty, which was more exposed due to a wind-enhanced low tide. Confederate sentinels onshore missed spotting the fortunate Cushing and his comrades.

At 7:40 the following evening, Cushing led a four-boat-party upstream to conduct a more thorough examination of Anderson's river channel barricade. Though shrouded by darkness, the closer inspection revealed an impressive double or triple line of wooden pilings, iron chains and ballast stone-filled cribs. The water defenses also comprised a number of buoyant torpedoes and mines attached to wooden frames submerged just below the river's surface. Elaborate British-manufactured fuze devices, called Wheatstone Exploders, were imported through the blockade to detonate the torpedoes from inside the fort. Cushing realized that both the mines and obstructions would seriously impede the U.S. Navy's attempt to ascend the Cape Fear River toward Wilmington.[46]

While studying the obstructions in the river, Cushing and his men heard loud cheering coming from inside Fort Anderson. The excitement of being so close to the enemy enticed Cushing to undertake greater risks. He landed his boats in Orton Cove (dubbed Cushing's Cove by the author) north of the fort and boldly crept down to the work. According to Cushing, none of his crew were willing to chance capture to view Rebel soldiers, so he went forward alone. Hiding just outside the fort's dirt and sod ramparts, the daring commando listened for some time to a rousing brass band, and then to "speeches being made by enthusiastic Confederates." One zealous officer in particular praised the gallantry of the troops, told them that the time had come to strike the final blow for Southern independence, and encouraged the soldiers to stand steadfast in the great struggle. "It was bright moonlight and I enjoyed the music in which the bombast was sandwiched," Cushing later recorded tongue in cheek.

As if finally recognizing the danger he faced, Cushing stole back to his anxious crew, who were still hidden with the boats in the marsh upstream. Reunited with their intrepid leader, the Federals quietly pulled their launches away from shore and headed downriver about 9:15 p.m. As they got abreast of the fort's high earthen walls, however, Confederate sentinels challenged them to halt. The Southerners had spotted the vessels as they entered Cushing's Cove earlier, and quickly alerted the officer of the day. An artillery crew was instructed to load their cannon with a stand of grapeshot and be ready to fire on the enemy boats as they emerged from their marshy hideout. The Confederates suspected the enemy sailors had come upriver to burn the supply steamer *Dawson* docked at Hills Landing about three miles north of Fort Anderson. "In a short while the boats were seen coming out of the cove and going down the river," recorded a Confederate soldier. A drummer beat the long roll calling the troops to action, and the cry: "Yankee boats in the river!" reverberated throughout the fort. Confederate soldiers rushed with their rifle-muskets to the batteries along the shoreline. "When [the enemy seamen] were about opposite the fort," observed one of Fort Anderson's defenders, "the order was given to fire."[47]

Under the withering fusillade, Cushing stood defiantly on the prow of his little boat and fired back at the fort with his Colt Navy revolver. "I succeeded in astonishing them; but the way the grape shot flew around, for awhile, from their guns was far from pleasant," Cushing admitted, "but night firing is very inaccurate and their

---

The cry, "Yankee boats in the river!" reverberated throughout the fort.

---

ammunition was wasted." Unscathed, the fortuitous commando and his cohorts vanished into the darkness, making their getaway to the warships anchored downriver by about 10:00 p.m. Never one to pass up an opportunity for self

WILMINGTON.

Exploits of the Gallant Commander Cushing.

The Town of Shallotte Captured and Much Property Destroyed.

Reconnoissance of the Wharves of Wilmington.

FORT ANDERSON LOOKED INTO,
&c.,   &c.,   &c.

Mr. Thomas M. Cook's Despatch.

FORT FISHER, Feb. 13, 1865.

A cold wind blowing strong from the north, and causing fresh water to conjeal wherever it was exposed, has compelled quietness up to this hour. How long this state of quietude will last I am unable to state, but I may guess not long. I shall not be surprised if my next despatch is dated from Wilmington.

Lieutenant Commander Cushing, of the navy, is the hero of several daring and gallant exploits of recent date, equal in meritorious character to the destruction of the ram Albemarle. On the 8th inst., acting under instruc-

The February 18, 1865 issue of the *New York Herald* ran a lengthy article on Lt. Cmdr. William B. Cushing's exploits at the Cape Fear, including his daring nocturnal visits to Fort Anderson. *New York Herald*

promotion, Cushing related his "adventure" in detail to war correspondents accompanying the navy, who promptly dispatched the exciting story north for publication. Cushing claimed that the speaker he had overheard inside Fort Anderson was none other than the Confederate commander of the Department of North Carolina himself, General Braxton Bragg. On February 18, just one week after the escapade, both the *New York Herald* and the *New York Tribune* carried articles describing Cushing's bold nighttime exploit. "The rising hero of the navy, Lieut. Cushing, continues to astonish the Rebels, as well as our own forces, by his acts of daring and skill," noted the *New York Tribune*.[48]

Not surprisingly, Cushing's version of his nocturnal visit to Fort Anderson differed considerably from the Southern version. The Union naval commando had indeed witnessed a Confederate pep rally at the Brunswick fort, which featured a performance by the Eutaw Band of the 25th South Carolina Infantry of Johnson Hagood's Brigade. The stirring speech that Cushing overheard, however, was not delivered by Braxton Bragg, as the Union naval officer had claimed, but by Lt. Col. John Douglas Taylor of the 36th North Carolina Regiment. Colonel John J. Hedrick of the 40th North Carolina had been called on to speak, but declined, asking Taylor to make an appearance in his stead. "The times being precarious and the spirit of despair everywhere abounding, I felt called upon to address my troops," Lieutenant Colonel Taylor recalled. The assembly was interrupted by the report of enemy boats in the river near the fort. Despite the Confederates' best efforts, the Union vessels managed to escape.

Three weeks later some of General Hoke's troops near Kinston captured a Union soldier who had a copy of the February 18, 1865 issue of the *New York Herald* newspaper containing the story of Cushing's exciting reconnaissance of Fort Anderson. The article reported in detail Lieutenant Colonel Taylor's oration to his Confederate soldiers. "[My] speech. . .was reported in the *New York Herald*," Taylor humorously boasted, "which incident is explained in the supposition that a Federal officer, supposed to have been Lieut. Cushing reconnoitering in an open boat, and was under the very guns of Anderson, and reported the speech." For the rest of his long life John Douglas Taylor enjoyed telling the story of his impromptu oration at Fort Anderson being published in a wartime Yankee newspaper.[49]

While Cushing and his companions scouted Fort Anderson by night, General Schofield proceeded with his plans for a daytime attack on the Brunswick stronghold. Before launching the assault on Anderson, however, Schofield determined to threaten Sugar Loaf two-and-a-half miles north of the Union lines on Federal Point. The department commander believed that pushing General Terry's corps, with Porter's warships in close support, toward Sugar Loaf "would compel [Hoke] to hold [his works] in force," and prevent him from detaching reinforcements to Fort Anderson, the real Federal target. Schofield hoped that a devastating bombardment of the Sugar Loaf lines by Porter's gunboats would enable Terry to overrun Hoke, and perhaps render an attack on Fort Anderson unnecessary. Even if Hoke held his position, the assault would give Schofield more time to bring up the remainder of his corps, which would be sent directly to the west side of the Cape Fear River for the advance on Fort Anderson.[50]

Schofield scheduled the Sugar Loaf assault for February 11. He instructed General Terry to "make a strong demonstration upon the enemy" and be ready to take Sugar Loaf if practicable; if not, to establish a defensive line near enough to threaten Hoke's position. Schofield called on Porter to provide Terry's assault force with covering fire by shelling both Sugar Loaf and Fort Anderson. Still trying to shake-off their sea legs after the long and stormy voyage down the Carolina coast, Cox's troops would be held in reserve during the assault. Porter grumbled his disapproval of Schofield's plan. In his opinion, even if the Federals "succeeded in dislodging the [Rebels], they would retreat by roads known only to themselves and leave [Union troops] in possession of barren sand hills and large numbers of killed and wounded." Despite his mis-

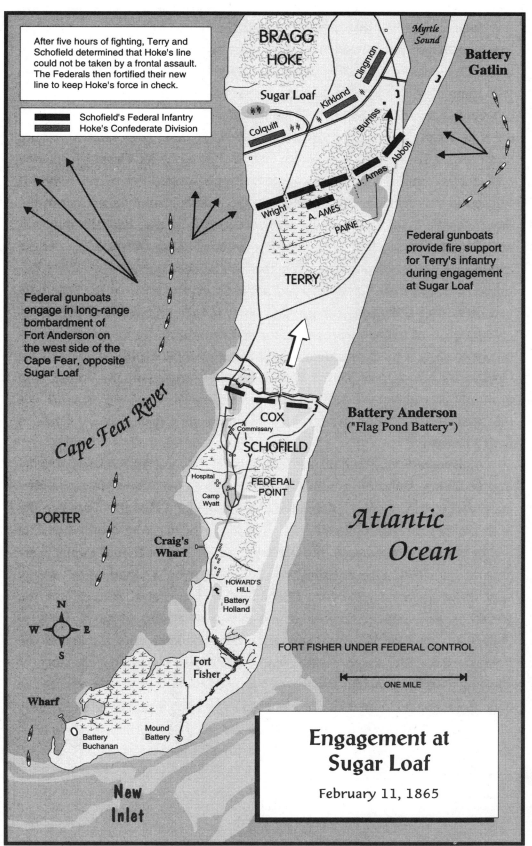

After five hours of fighting, Terry and Schofield determined that Hoke's line could not be taken by a frontal assault. The Federals then fortified their new line to keep Hoke's force in check.

▬▬▬ Schofield's Federal Infantry
▬▬▬ Hoke's Confederate Division

BRAGG
HOKE
Sugar Loaf
Clingman
Kirkland
Burriss
Colquitt
Myrtle Sound
Battery Gatlin
Wright
A. AMES
J. Ames
Abbott
PAINE
TERRY

Federal gunboats provide fire support for Terry's infantry during engagement at Sugar Loaf

Federal gunboats engage in long-range bombardment of Fort Anderson on the west side of the Cape Fear, opposite Sugar Loaf

Cape Fear River

COX
Commissary
SCHOFIELD
FEDERAL POINT
Hospital
Camp Wyatt

Battery Anderson ("Flag Pond Battery")

Atlantic Ocean

PORTER

Craig's Wharf

HOWARD'S HILL
Battery Holland

FORT FISHER UNDER FEDERAL CONTROL

N
W   E
S

Fort Fisher

ONE MILE

Wharf

Mound Battery
Battery Buchanan

Engagement at Sugar Loaf

February 11, 1865

New Inlet

Mark A. Moore

givings, Porter reluctantly fell in with Schofield's plans.[51]

By February 11, General Terry's soldiers were eager for a fight. It had been a month since they had captured Fort Fisher, and they were anxious for relief from the monotony of sand, surf, and salt water. While Terry's infantry of the XXIV and XXV Army Corps battled their way toward Sugar Loaf, Porter's warships began their bombardment. Gunboats on the Atlantic side of Federal Point opened the day's fighting about 9:00 a.m. An hour later the *Mackinaw* and *Unadilla* on the Cape Fear River commenced firing on both Sugar Loaf and Fort Anderson. The gunboats unleashed a long range, slow paced fire on Anderson designed to distract the attention of its garrison from the Union attack on Federal Point. About noon the Brunswick defenders responded, but their cannon fire was weak and largely ineffective. Even so, the *Mackinaw* was hit by two Whitworth bolts—"vis-

itors," a Union sailor called them—one tearing through the smoke pipe and the other damaging the main gaff.[52]

The chaos of battle affected at least one Union sailor on the receiving end of the Confederate projectiles. "It is a very easy and pleasant thing for one to sit at his comfortable home and read of shelling forts and running batteries, and say what the Navy ought and must perform," he observed, "but I assure you it is not so pleasant to come down here amidst the plunging shot and screaming shells, deadly torpedoes, sharp shooters, and fight your way to Wilmington."[53]

Helping the U.S. Navy fight its way toward Wilmington was the monitor *Montauk*, which joined the Fort Anderson bombardment about 11:00 a.m., and maintained her shelling until dark on February 11. The ironclad's armor plating and low profile allowed her to engage the earthen fort from closer range—about 1,000

The U.S. double-ender gunboat *Mackinaw* and the monitor *Montauk* on the Cape Fear River shell Fort Anderson on February 11, 1865, in support of a Union attack against Confederate forces entrenched at Sugar Loaf on the opposite shore from the Brunswick bastion. One observer noted that "[the *Montauk's* 300-pound] shells fell into and around the Fort in a very lively manner." *Harper's Weekly, March 4, 1865*

yards out—than the wooden gunboats. Furthermore, the experience the monitor's gunners had acquired in the siege of Charleston enabled them to place most of their 15-inch cannonballs on or inside the fort's walls. "The ironclad has but one 15-inch gun, and is handled very well," noted an impressed Confederate soldier. "Her [300 pound] shells fell into and around the Fort in a very lively manner." A Northern journalist marvelled at the precision of the *Montauk's* fire: "Every shot struck with the most remarkable accuracy. One after another they glanced along [the fort's] ramparts or burst on its glacis, sending the sand in clouds to the sky."[54]

From his vantage point along the west bank of Federal Point, General Cox watched the duel between the *Montauk* and Fort Anderson. He was amused by the sight of some sailors who stood on the monitor's deck to inspect the effect of her fire, but were occasionally forced to take refuge behind her revolving turret when Confederate counter-shots came too close. The ironclad's deck was almost flush with the river's surface, offering Confederate artillerymen virtually no target. Still, some of the Southerners' shots ricocheted off the monitor's armored turret or passed perilously close by. Even the ones that hit, however, did little damage. "We struck it often during the day," one Confederate cannoneer claimed, "[but] our balls

Previously unpublished portrait of Capt. Charles F. Bahnson, Chief of Transportation at Fort Anderson, who recalled the U.S. Navy's "missiles of death" that fell on the Brunswick fort on February 11, 1865. *Courtesy of Sarah Bahnson Chapman*

would bound from it like shooting marbles against a brick wall."[55]

The U.S. Navy's long-range bombardment of Fort Anderson kept its defenders hugging the earthworks for protection, though most of the shells burst harmlessly on the terre plain or beyond. "The Parade Ground bears evidence of some missiles of death having dropped close in that vicinty, but no damage is done," remarked Capt. Charles F. Bahnson, Chief of Transportation at Fort Anderson. "One 15-inch shell dropped close to a house in which I formerly stayed, but now occupied by Maj. [William A.] Holland [40th North Carolina], and being nearly spent, rolled against the house, with just enough force to rebound to the distance of a few feet, and lay there quietly without exploding."[56]

The Union projectiles caused as few casualties among Fort Anderson's defenders as they caused serious damage to the earthen defenses. Reportedly, only one soldier was wounded, suffering a slight injury to his heel. Even so, the Confederates admitted they did "some tall dodging" to escape the incoming naval shells. "There were many narrow escapes from pieces [of projectiles], which were plentifully distributed," claimed Lt. Zaccheus Ellis of Company B, 1st Battalion North Carolina Heavy Artillery. Yet Admiral Porter was satisfied with the results of his bombardment, for it had succeeded in preventing the Confederates from shelling Terry's troops advancing on Federal Point.[57]

Despite Porter's contentment with the navy's performance at Fort Anderson, Hoke's Confederates held firm at Sugar Loaf. After hours of heavy skirmishing, a frustrated Alfred H. Terry concluded that neither his infantry nor Porter's gunboats were going to dislodge Hoke's strongly entrenched veterans. With his troops exposed to a steady fire and casualties mounting, Terry decided to dig in, entrenching his brigades about 900 yards south of Hoke's fortifications. General Schofield joined Terry at the front late in the afternoon on February 11 and concurred with his opinion that Hoke's line probably could not be overrun by a frontal assault. Despite this grim assessment, Schofield believed that the day's fighting had been advantageous to the Unionists. A new line had been established close enough to Sugar Loaf to keep Hoke in check. Given the hard-pressed nature of Terry's thrust—and the proximity of the Federals' main force—Hoke surely could not afford to dispatch reinforcements to Fort Anderson, thereby weakening his own division on Federal Point. Ironically, the Federal advantage gained in the face of stubborn Confederate resistance also made Schofield uneasy about dividing his command to strike Fort Anderson. Should he split his army in the face of such opposition?[58]

Schofield's dilemma was diverted, at least temporarily, when the expeditionary force's chief engineer, Bvt. Brig. Gen. Cyrus Comstock, reported that he had found a weakness in Hoke's defenses. As Terry's infantrymen attacked Sugar Loaf, Comstock reconnoitered up the beach and discovered that the Confederates' left flank on Myrtle Sound could be turned. A long, narrow tongue of sand that snaked up the coast separating the sound from the ocean (present-day Masonboro Island), skirted Hoke's left side. With the shoreline open, Comstock believed that a swift, secret movement could put troops in the rear of Hoke's position. The chief engineer proposed to march a force under cover of darkness up the beach in an effort to outflank the Sugar Loaf line.[59]

General Schofield considered the plan "quite practicable," and agreed to try it after a more thorough reconnaisance of Fort Anderson suggested that capturing it by frontal assault was going to be a difficult task. In all likelihood, Fort Anderson could not be taken without bypassing Orton Pond on the fort's far western end. Furthermore, time was of less concern for Schofield after he received word that Sherman's advance through South Carolina had been impeded by heavy rains and flooded roads. Schofield authorized Comstock to attempt his flanking operation.[60]

The change in plans sowed additional tension within the ranks of the Federal high command. Admiral Porter was infuriated when he got word of Comstock's beach expedition. Privately, he accused Schofield of reversing the agreed-upon plan to attack Fort Anderson once General Grant was back in Virginia. Porter considered it "imbecile" to attack by the beach. Yet the generally outspoken admiral held his tongue and readied his ships, which would transfer some troops up the coastline for the operation.[61]

On two nights, February 12 and 14, Comstock attempted to maneuver Union troops into Hoke's rear, but foul weather halted both advances. Exhausted by all the marching and countermarching along Myrtle Sound beach and soaked to the bone by cold drenching rains, General Cox's soldiers preferred shooting their way into Wilmington. General Schofield sensed his troops' frustration and finally resolved to adopt the original plan of attacking Wilmington by way of Fort Anderson. With a hint of respect for the Cape Fear's stubborn gray-clad troops, one Unionist commented: "The Confederacy was about to tumble, but they are blind to the fact."[62]

Chapter 3

The Battle

After leading several reconnaissances into Brunswick County, Lt. Col. Albert M. Barney of the 142nd New York Infantry (shown here in a previously unpublished photo), reported that Union operations against Fort Anderson would be hampered by the piney lowlands, marshy ponds and cypress swamps that surrounded the Confederate bastion. *Author's Collection*

Reinforcements from General Schofield's Second Division, en route from Alexandria, Virginia, reached the Lower Cape Fear on February 14. The first of these troops were the 23rd Michigan Infantry of Col. Orlando Moore's Second Brigade, and 100 men of the 26th Kentucky Infantry, temporarily attached to the Second Brigade from the First Brigade. The balance of the Second Brigade was in transport close behind. The arrival of additional men was welcomed by Schofield, as it eased his apprehension about dividing his army to operate on both sides of the Cape Fear River. He immediately sent the Michigan and Kentucky troops to Smithville and made arrangements with Admiral Porter to transfer General Cox's Third Division from Federal Point across the river to attack Fort Anderson. Schofield also ordered yet another reconnaissance of the fort's approaches.[1]

Lieutenant Colonel Albert M. Barney of the 142nd New York Infantry, commanding officer at Smithville, led a scouting party of 300 men in the direction of Fort Anderson on February 15. Barney marched his men out of Smithville toward the powerful Confederate earthen defenses, but was prevented from reaching the fort by enemy vedettes of the 2nd South Carolina Cavalry. The Palmetto State horsemen checked Barney's reconnaissance force in a lively skirmish at White Spring's Branch, three miles north of the town. Unable to penetrate the cavalry screen, Barney's New Yorkers spent most of the rainy day examining the area surrounding the fort. Despite Barney's hopes to the contrary, the countryside was not suitable for a full-scale military operation. Instead of accessible terrain, the Federals found the ground south of Fort Anderson filled with piney lowlands interlaced with creeks, marshy ponds and cypress swamps. While the topography was difficult, the mainland still offered more room to maneuver than Federal Point, an advantage—along with the army's numerical superiority and the navy's firepower—that Schofield meant to exploit in his effort to capture Fort Anderson. At the very least, despite frequent rains Barney could report that the roads remained in reasonably good condition.[2]

While the recent heavy rains had little affect on Brunswick County's roads, they did manage to delay the transfer of General Cox's division from Federal Point to Smithville until February 16. Throughout that day the expeditionary force's chief quartermaster, Col. George S. Dodge, supervised the movement of troops, field artillery and supply wagons on board the steamers *Nansemond, Eolus, Wilderness,* and *Moccasin* across the harbor. The remainder of the Second Brigade, commanded by Col. Orlando H. Moore, finally arrived from the north and joined Cox's command at Smithville. The only artillery of Cox's division that had

arrived thus far was Battery D, 1st Ohio Regiment Light Artillery, along with Colonel Moore's infantrymen who had disembarked two days earlier. Added to the units on hand, the Ohio artillerists together with the 23rd Michigan and the 26th Kentucky rounded out the force of about 6,000 troops that would assault Fort Anderson. The Federals encamped for the night about half-a-mile west of Smithville and prepared for battle.[3]

Jacob Cox began his march toward Fort Anderson, nine miles upriver from Smithville, about 8:00 a.m. the next morning, February 17. Lem Brown and other blacks familiar with the back roads of Brunswick County served as guides for the advancing Federals. The march on the sandy Wilmington Road, while slow going, was initially uneventful. One soldier reported travelling through "country that was

Previously unpublished image of Col. George S. Dodge, chief quartermaster of the expeditionary force in the Wilmington Campaign. Dodge directed the transfer of General Cox's division from Federal Point across the Cape Fear River to Smithville (seen here) on February 16, 1865, for the attack on Fort Anderson. *Author's Collection*

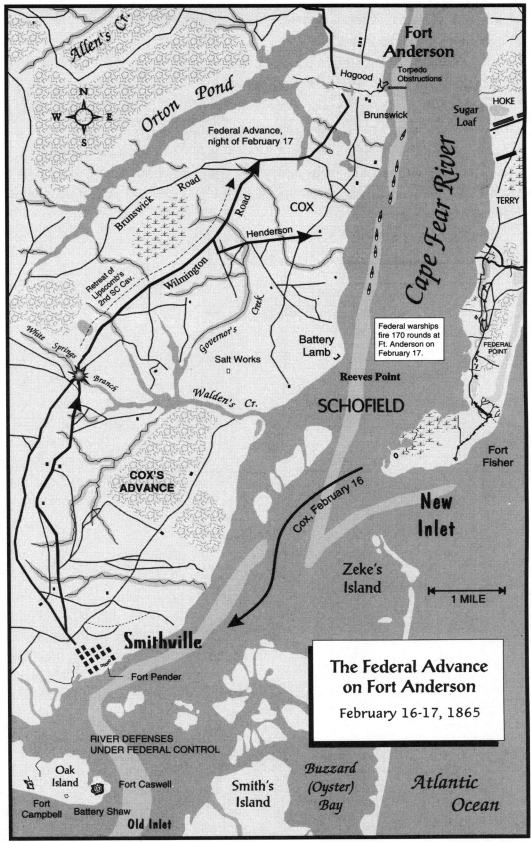

The Federal Advance on Fort Anderson

February 16-17, 1865

Mark A. Moore

nearly level and had a sickly growth of pines which had been boxed for turpentine." The few inhabitants who lived along the route gaped from the doors of their cabins as Mr. Lincoln's army tromped past. Most of them had never seen Union soldiers before. The slaves "came running out. . .singing and shouting with joy and thanksgiving," glad to see that, contrary to what their white masters had told them, Yankee soldiers did not have horns and tails. Some of the overjoyed blacks rushed forward to embrace the soldiers, while others dropped to their knees in prayer, fully aware that the blue-clad troops heralded their freedom. An Illinois soldier described it as "both an affecting and laughable scene—a prayer meeting and a circus combined."[4]

But the amused Federal troops were soon reminded that the grim business of war was still at hand when Confederate cavalry attacked them about three miles outside of Smithville.

Colonel John S. "Jack" Casement's Second Brigade of Jacob Cox's division comprised five regiments of blue-uniformed rifle-musket bearers from Illinois, Indiana, Ohio and Tennessee in the advance on Fort Anderson. *U.S. Army Military History Institute*

For most of the day the 2nd South Carolina Cavalry harassed the Union column, staging hit-and-run raids, setting fire to the woods, and felling trees across the road to retard the Federals' advance. The armed gray-clad riders made a brief stand at Governor's Creek, but were quickly turned aside by Cox's skirmish line, three companies of the 16th Kentucky Infantry of Col. Oscar W. Sterl's First Brigade.[5]

Near Governor's Creek the road forked, prompting General Cox to split his army to cover both avenues of advance. Cox accompanied Col. Thomas J. Henderson's Third Brigade on a byroad leading in the direction of the Cape Fear River, while Oscar Sterl's, Jack Casement's, and Orlando Moore's units continued their movement up the Wilmington Road. Late that afternoon Cox and Henderson struck the river about two miles below Fort Anderson and opened communications with Admiral Porter. General Schofield was also on the river, having established his command post on board the medical steamer *S.R. Spaulding.* From that vantage point, Schofield believed he could best coordinate the movements of both Cox's and Terry's forces—now totalling some 15,000 troops—on both sides of the waterway. As soon as Cox made contact, however, Schofield went ashore to join him.[6]

Some of Porter's warships had been battling Fort Anderson's batteries all afternoon in an effort to distract the Confederates' attention from Cox's advance. The monitor *Montauk* led a group of five gunboats upstream shortly after midday. The ironclad assumed a position about 1,000 yards off the fort where, under a "pretty brisk" shelling from Confederate artillery, she opened fire. "The enemy did not allow the *Montauk* to take her position so near the fort without molestation," reported a Union journalist. Fear of torpedoes in the channel and not Confederate cannon fire, however, dissuaded

The *U.S.S. Maratanza* joined six other gunboats in the river bombardment of Fort Anderson on February 17, 1865, in an effort to shield the approach of Cox's Union infantry. *U.S. Army Military History Institute*

the *Montauk*'s commander, Lt. Cmdr. Edward E. Stone, from attempting to push his ship much closer to the enemy's belching guns.[7]

The *Pawtuxet, Lenapee, Pequot, Unadilla,* and *Maratanza* cautiously took up their battle stations behind the monitor amid the incoming Southern projectiles. The Confederates subjected the approaching Union ships to a steady and deadly cannonade. Only minutes after the *Pequot* took up her position, a whistling Whitworth bolt crashed into one of her stanchions (an upright support beam). Flying splinters struck five sailors, mortally wounding Quartermaster William Brain in the stomach, and severely injuring Quatermaster Jer. Lyons and Ordinary Seaman Carl Poelstrom. Lyons' nasty wound required the amputation of his left arm, while Poelstrom lost a foot to the surgeon's saw.

Near the front of the naval battle line, the *Lenapee* was splashed by a tall column of water thrown up by a Confederate ball that plunged into the river just shy of the gunboat. The near hit prompted Lt. Cmdr. John S. Barnes to move the *Lenapee* back downriver a bit, beyond the range of the Southerners' artillery. Other warships followed suit. Once they were finally anchored in position by 3:15 p.m., the gunboats began a long range bombardment of the fort. The river's narrow channel forced most of the gunboats to fire over their bows, instead of employing their broadside artillery as the navy had done so effectively at Fort Fisher. Admiral Porter had issued explicit instructions for the warships to concentrate their fire against the fort and its artillery, and not to be tempted to fire on the enemy's flags, which were more visible targets. Shortly after 5:00 o'clock the *Little Ada,* a former blockade runner converted into a gunboat, steamed up and joined the battle.[8]

With most of the Union warships out of range of Fort Anderson's seacoast guns, the Confederates concentrated their fire on the *Montauk*. They aimed forty-seven shots at the ironclad, but the 32-pound solid iron cannonballs that hit their mark could not penetrate the monitor's thick iron plating. "The *Montauk* received her fire with perfect indifference," remarked a war correspondent. Another observer noted that "not a person was injured on board the presuming monitor, although she was hit over and over again in every part of her, nor was the vessel damaged in the slightest degree." Some of the other vessels sustained minor damage, however. Fortunately for the flotilla, the Confederates' 12-pounder

Whitworth rifle soon depleted its limited ammunition supply and was withdrawn from the battle. The British-made rifle-gun remained mute throughout most of the exchange on February 17, unable to fire so much as a single round.[9]

The Southern cannon which had been active fell silent as the Union ships withdrew after dark. General Hagood had refrained from firing most of his 32-pounders because the gunboats were well beyond their range, and there was no point in wasting valuable ammunition. The firepower and positioning of these cannon caused Hagood no little worry. Of Fort Anderson's nine heavy guns, only "two. . .were rifled but not banded," observed Hagood, "and their carriages were old and worn, and bore across and down the river. No gun could be brought to bear up the river," he lamented, "and consequently, if any portion of the fleet should have passed the fort we would have had to fire upon it, while it would have taken nearly every gun in reverse."

The gunboats attempted no such maneuver, however. They stopped shelling after sunset and dropped back downstream. The Union naval bombardment of Fort Anderson proved to be little more than a wasteful exercise. The Federal warships had fired only 170 projectiles at the fort in about four hours, causing little damage to the works and wounding only one defender. More importantly, the bombardment had failed to disguise Cox's advance: General Hagood was well aware of the Federal army's approach.[10]

Just as the Union gunboats were ending their fitful exchange with Hagood's artillery, Cox and Henderson on the riverbank reestablished contact with Sterl's, Casement's and Moore's brigades to the west on the Wilmington Road. The soldiers had advanced more than seven miles and had skirmished almost continuously during the day. Cox ordered his men to throw out a picket line and then entrenched his force about a mile-and-a-half south of Fort Anderson. As the sound of shovels and axes reverberated in the growing darkness, the scene in the piney woods took on a slightly macbre air. Earlier in the day Confederate cavalry had set fires in the woods which, fueled by strong winds, continued to burn well into the night. "Acres and acres of forest were wrapped in vived flames [and] the sky was aglow with the reflection of the great fire," noted one observer. As the fires crackled and burned around them, the Federals tried to get some rest. They slept on their firearms that night, knowing that the next day would bring a different kind of fire.[11]

As their soldiers dozed, Generals Schofield and Cox spent the evening plotting to take Fort

As their soldiers dozed, Generals Schofield and Cox spent the evening plotting to take Fort Anderson.

Anderson. It appeared that the navy would be unable to bring enough heavy ordnance to bear on the fort's elevated batteries to silence them, primarily because the river channel was too narrow and full of obstructions and torpedoes. While the gunboats could provide long range fire, their shelling would have to be delivered beyond the effective range of the warships. "The channel is so narrow that but one vessel can operate at a time," explained a Union naval officer. No one doubted that it would take longer to knock out the fort's ordnance than it had at Fort Fisher, especially since there were fewer ships and guns to do the work. It was also possible that, despite its best efforts, the navy would not be able to silence the fort's artillery at all. The brunt of responsibility for Fort

Anderson's capture seemingly rested on the shoulders of the U.S. Army.[12]

With that assessment in mind, Schofield instructed Cox to make a reconnaissance-in-force of Fort Anderson the following morning. After a close inspection of the work they would decide how best to proceed. If the naval fire—which Porter would resume in the morning—had destroyed or dismounted the fort's artillery, then Cox should be able to storm the works. If not, Cox was to entrench two of his brigades south of the fort and then make a forced march with his two remaining brigades to the west end of Orton Pond. There he would be joined by Bvt. Maj. Gen. Adelbert Ames' division, which Schofield would bring over from Federal Point. With this combined force, Cox would sweep around Orton Pond and attack Fort Anderson from the rear, while his two entrenched brigades threatened from in front. At the same time, Admiral Porter's gunboats would maintain a steady fire on the fort and Terry's force would continue to press General Hoke's Confederates on Federal Point.[13]

Saturday, February 18, dawned pleasant at the Cape Fear, promising a third consecutive day of good weather. By the time the sun was high in the sky, the mid-winter's day was balmy

> *Corporal Stitt kept the Confederate bullet that had struck him as a "souvenir of the war, and as a reminder of his 'close call.'"*

and even warm. General Cox deployed his division in the smouldering woodlands and advanced about 7:00 a.m., with Henderson's brigade moving up the riverbank, Casement's unit taking the center, and Sterl's anchoring the left of the line. Moore's brigade followed in echelon in the rear.

Within an hour Federal sharpshooters encountered Confederate pickets and the fighting quickly developed across the front. "As daylight advanced the [scattered discharges of musketry] became more earnest, and soon it became apparent that our forces were pressing the enemy into their works," recorded a journalist accompanying the Union advance on Fort Anderson. The "press" came at a cost for the Federal troops. Eleven soldiers of the 65th Indiana Infantry of Jack Casement's brigade were wounded on the skirmish line during the day. The only reported casualty of the 112th Illinois Infantry of Thomas Henderon's brigade, however, was Cpl. James Stitt of Company D. A musket ball pierced his pocket watch before causing a severe wound to his groin. Convinced that his pocket watch, although destroyed, had saved his life, Corporal Stitt kept the Confederate bullet that had struck him as a "souvenir of the war, and as a reminder of his 'close call.'"[14]

The popping of small arms fire to the south brought Hagood's Confederates inside Fort Anderson to their trenches in expectation of an enemy assault. "Skirmishing going on and every one on the 'qui vive,'" remarked Abram Clement of the 11th South Carolina Infantry. About 9:00 a.m., General Hagood ordered his skirmish line to fall back. Within a short time the vastly outnumbered riflemen, who had been conducting the stubborn inch-by-inch retreat, withdrew into view of the fort's walls. Many of the skirmishers took up new positions in a line of rifle pits 200 yards south of the main works. Some of the "gopher holes," as the soldiers referred to the rifle pits, were carved out of the ballast stone basements of Brunswick Town's crumbled dwellings close to the river's edge.[15]

The Confederates closest to the Cape Fear River were exposed to heavy fire from both Henderson's skirmishers and Porter's warships,

This engraving, which appeared in *Frank Leslie's Illustrated Newspaper*, is one of only two known wartime views of Fort Anderson. While he exaggerated the fort's features and armament, sketch artist Joseph Becker did manage to capture the strength and extent of the Brunswick defenses along the riverfront. *Frank Leslie's Illustrated Newspaper*

which had recently joined the escalating fight. Unable to maintain their position under the thunderous fire, the Southerners scurried into the fort for safety. Their retreat created a gap on the firing line which enabled Henderson's lead regiment, the 65th Indiana Infantry, to advance through some soggy ground to within 300 yards of the fort. Although armed with rapid-fire 16-shot Henry rifles, the Hoosiers did not remain at the front for long. Misdirected projectiles from the Union gunboats wounded some Indiana soldiers and compelled the rest to break for the rear.[16]

While the skirmishing increased in intensity and huge naval shells arched toward the fort, General Cox moved his brigades to within 600 yards of the fort and, together with General Schofield, surveyed the terrain. An impenetrable swamp and creek fed into the river near the fort's main batteries in front of the Federals' right flank, the same area recently vacated by the Hoosiers who had suffered the friendly fire

of Porter's gunboats. The ground on the Union left-center and far left, however, was more open—especially along the Wilmington Road, which bisected the fort's sand curtain. About 300 yards of scrub oaks and piney timber, which at one time had fronted the fort's mammoth walls, had been slashed and burned by the Confederates to provide clear fields of fire. While abatis (sharpened stakes) emplaced near the fort's ramparts would make an infantry attack more difficult, the open ground also provided Schofield and Cox with a good view of Fort Anderson and its impressive features.[17]

The long shank of the "L"—which faced the Federals to the south—was a crooked feature that took advantage of the broken terrain. Confederate engineers ran the earthworks up to the edge of (and partially behind) two fresh water ponds located about 250 yards apart midway down the line. This sage engineering feat allowed the defenders to utilize the ponds like giant moats. The earthen walls on the fort's far

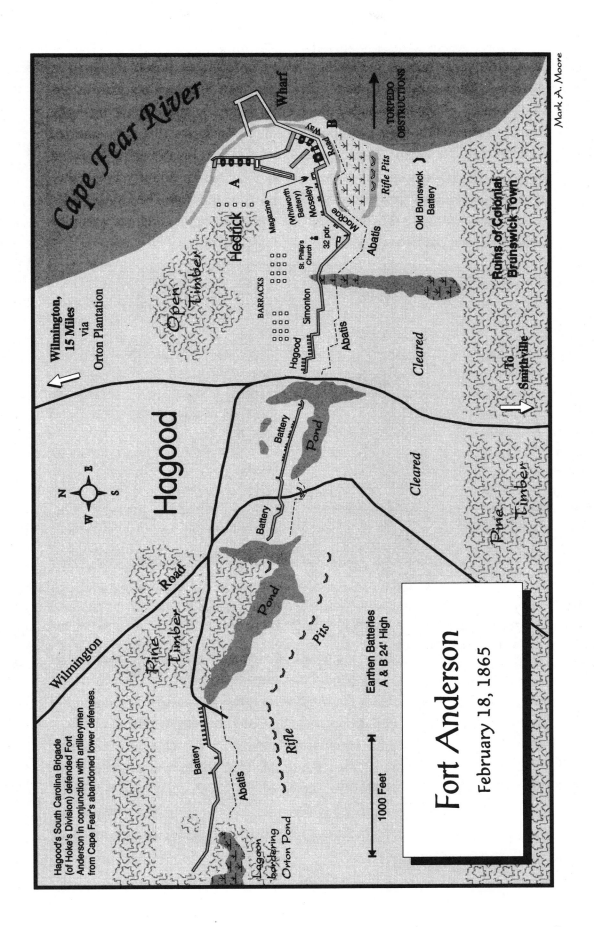

Mark A. Moore

Hagood's South Carolina Brigade (of Hoke's Division) defended Fort Anderson in conjunction with artillerymen from Cape Fear's abandoned lower defenses.

Cape Fear River

Wilmington, 15 Miles via Orton Plantation

Open Timber

Hedrick

Wharf

Way

B

Road

TORPEDO OBSTRUCTIONS

Rifle Pits

Moseley (Whitworth Battery)

Magazine

MacRae

Abatis

Old Brunswick Battery

A

St. Philip's Church

32 pdr.

BARRACKS

Simonton

Cleared

Hagood

Abatis

Ruins of Colonial Brunswick Town

To Smithville

Hagood

Battery

Pond

N E S W

Battery

Cleared

Pine Timber

Wilmington

Pine Timber

Road

Pond

Pits

Rifle

Earthen Batteries A & B 24' High

1000 Feet

Fort Anderson
February 18, 1865

Battery

Abatis

Lagoon bordering Orton Pond

western end were constructed behind and against a deep cypress swamp, which itself fed into Orton Pond. Abatis, epaulments, ditches, tiny ponds, swampy bogs, and rifle pits further strengthened the fort's land face, while light artillery—strategically placed along the mile-long stretch—enjoyed "full play" over the field of fire across the ground in front. The terrain occupied by the defenders behind (north of) the fort's walls was similar to that beyond its front: cleared fields and wooded stands of pine trees, turkey and scrub oaks, and interlacing patches of swampy ground. The Confederates had also utilized a small redoubt, Old Brunswick Battery, near the main fort, but reportedly had abandoned it as the Federals approached.

Fort Anderson's Achilles' Heel, as Schofield and Cox (and Hagood) already knew, was its wide open rear area. The fort could be outflanked by simply going around the west end of Orton Pond, where the Confederates had neglected to build adequate defenses. A flanking move around the mill pond, however, would mean a twelve-mile detour for the Federals.[18]

After surveying the imposing defenses before him, however, Schofield concluded that the enveloping maneuver around Orton Pond was the best plan for capturing Fort Anderson, and he ordered Cox to undertake it. To disguise his intentions, Cox requested that Admiral Porter intensify his shore bombardment, while Colonels Moore and Henderson demonstrated with their infantry brigades across Hagood's front. Under Schofield's orders, Moore and Henderson entrenched their units inside the tree line 600 yards from the fort before advancing a strong force of skirmishers—the 63rd Indiana Infantry from Henderson's brigade, among other units—into the burned open fields in front. The long-anticipated enemy thrust provoked a sharp reply from Southern defenders when the Federals advanced toward the line of Confederate rifle pits just outside Fort

Anderson's main wall. The thin line of Confederate defenders was supported by two field batteries (Capt. William Badham, Jr.'s Company B, 3rd Battalion North Carolina Light Artillery and Capt. Abner A. Moseley's Sampson Artillery) which opened "a very vigorous fire with artillery and shelled [the Federals] quite briskly for several hours." There was also some close quarter fighting as the Federal soldiers slowly advanced. A Union war correspondent later reported that "during the skirmishing [a] Lieutenant Laswell of the 65th Indiana was [made] a prisoner for a few minutes, when his company charged and recaptured him."[19]

As Moore's and Henderson's troops moved into position—pushing Hagood's skirmishers inside the fort in the process—Cox assembled Casement's and Sterl's brigades and the 1st Ohio Artillery battery, commanded by Lt. Cecil Reed, for his flanking force. Guided by a local black man, the brigades started out about 2:00 p.m. on February 18, advancing westward along the Brunswick Road (also called the British Road) that skirted the south edge of Orton Pond. General Hagood was unaware of Cox's movement, though he was cognizant of Fort Anderson's weak right flank. He had posted a detachment of the 2nd South Carolina Cavalry at the far end of Orton Pond to warn him of any attempt by the enemy to turn that flank.[20]

With few defensive options, Hagood ordered his gunners and infantry to blast away at the Union troops immediately south of the fort. The commanding general fully expected a Union frontal assault against his works at any time. "Skirmishing going on in front of our lines; a large force of the enemy in our front, we expecting our works to be charged every minute," recorded one of Fort Anderson's nervous defenders. To dissuade the Federals from making the attempt, the Confederates kept up an intense fusillade of musketry and field artillery fire for most of the day. Captain Moseley's and Captain Badham's batteries on the right of the

During the hottest part of the fighting at Fort Anderson on February 18, 1865, the drum and bugle corps of the 104th Ohio Infantry kept up a constant serenade of patriotic music for their comrades in blue. Not to be outdone, the brass band of the 25th South Carolina Infantry in the fort answered the Ohio musicians song for song.   *N.C. Division of Archives and History*

line laid down a heavy fire on the advancing Union infantry.[21]

A Union officer commented that the Confederate artillery barrage was "the most accurate shelling [he had] ever witnessed from rebel batteries." One Federal infantryman, Cpl. Theodore J. Wagner of Company A, 23rd Michigan, noted that "the enemy shelled us all day & we lost qite a number of the regt." Under the deluge of Southern iron and lead, the Federals quickly dug in for safety. "Officers and men vied with each other in throwing up breastworks with whatever they could bring into requisition," noted an eyewitness, "tin plates, cups, sticks, and hands were kept very busy until a sufficient temporary protection was formed." Spades and shovels were brought up from Smithville and the men spent most of the afternoon strengthening their breastworks amid the whizzing projectiles.[22]

During the height of the fierce fighting, the drum and bugle corps of the 104th Ohio Infantry of Oscar Sterl's brigade entertained the Union combatants with "a constant serenade of patriotic music." Strangely, Confederate sol-

diers inside the fort could hear the music wafting above the roar of artillery and small arms fire. Not to be outdone, they employed a brass band of their own—the Eutaw Band of the 25th South Carolina Infantry—to play Southern melodies. Like their Confederate counterparts, Union troops heard the strains of martial airs above the din of battle, including one recognizable tune, "Who's Been Here While I've Been Gone." The battling bands attempted to inspire their comrades in the thick of the fight, or perhaps to dilute its insanity.[23]

As the hours passed and the expected Union infantry attack failed to materialize, Hagood, perhaps suspecting that the enemy effort south of the fort was a feint, ordered his infantry back out onto the skirmish line.

Despite the heavy musketry and exploding projectiles, neither army experienced any significant losses. The Federals sustained only about twenty casualties. Most of those were members of the 65th Indiana Infantry, who had experienced heavy action on the skirmish line that morning. Michael Reinhart of the 65th Indiana's Company H was hit in the face by a projectile, J.S. Brayfield of Company I had his leg broken, and Thomas G. Horton of Company K was severely wounded in the thigh during the melee. Soldiers from other western regiments suffered similar injuries. General Schofield narrowly escaped harm when a Confederate shell exploded near him as he galloped along the line supervising his troops. Colonel Oliver L. Spaulding, commander of the 23rd Michigan Infantry of Orlando Moore's brigade, also had a close call. A projectile struck a sapling under which he was standing, and shook the tree so violently that it knocked Spaulding to the ground.[24]

Union naval losses were also light. William Wilson, captain of the forecastle on the *Chippewa*, was killed and Ordinary Seaman Daniel Lund lost his left arm by incoming Confederate cannonballs. Admiral Porter later reported that his total losses were three killed and four wounded. One Union sailor, however, claimed that a tragic accident and not Southern iron caused most of the U.S. Navy's losses during the day. At nightfall a hawser on the *Lenapee* became fouled, and a detail was dispatched in a launch to clear it. As the sailors worked, the *Sassacus* inadvertently swung into the small boat, tipping it over and spilling its crew into the cold Cape Fear River. Four sailors allegedly drowned before rescue boats could reach them.[25]

Corporal Theodore J. Wagner of Company A, 23rd Michigan Infantry, wrote in his diary on February 18 that Confederate riflemen in Fort Anderson hit "qite a number" of his regiment during the battle. *Courtesy of Dick and Ellen McMann*

About half of Porter's flotilla engaged Fort Anderson on February 18. At the first sound of musketry onshore early that morning, Admiral Porter ordered his warships into action. The *Montauk* again led the flotilla upstream. Fifteen other vessels—the *Sassacus*, *Lenapee*, *Mackinaw*, *Huron*, *Pontoosuc*, *Maratanza*, *Unadilla*, *Pawtuxet*, *Osceola*, *Shawmut*, *Seneca*, *Nyack*, *Chippewa*, *Little Ada*, and the *Malvern*—followed the ironclad. The Confederate shore batteries fired the opening shots as the Union gunboats took up their battle stations shortly after 8:00 a.m.

Testing both the river obstructions and the effectiveness of the fort's arsenal, the *Montauk* crept to within 800 yards of the fort, 200 yards closer than the previous day. As expected, the narrow channel restricted the movement of the remainder of the gunboats, forcing them to line up and down the waterway about a mile or so south of the fort. Admiral Porter steamed about in the *Malvern* personally directing the deployment and fire of his warships. By noon the warships were all in position and began shelling the enemy's defenses. The river was as smooth as glass, enabling the ships to quickly establish their range of fire. "The ves-

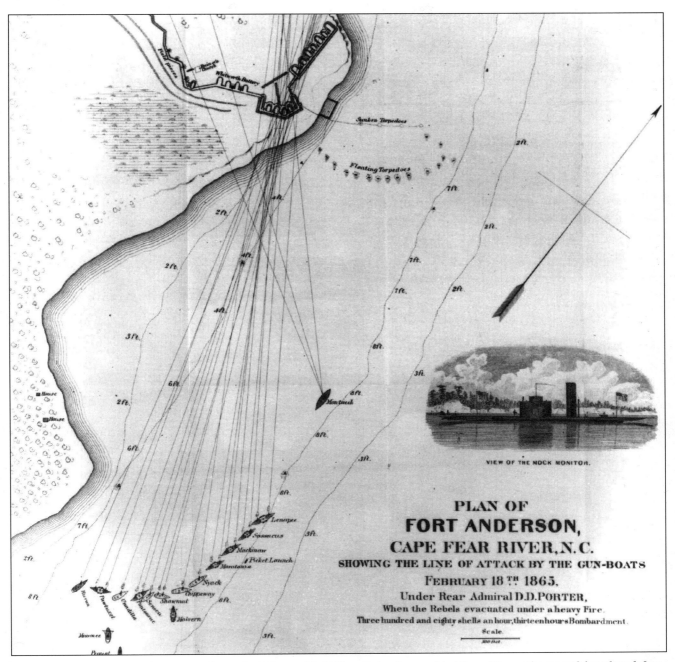

VIEW OF THE MOCK MONITOR.

PLAN OF
FORT ANDERSON,
CAPE FEAR RIVER, N.C.
SHOWING THE LINE OF ATTACK BY THE GUN-BOATS
FEBRUARY 18TH 1865,
Under Rear Admiral D.D.PORTER,
When the Rebels evacuated under a heavy Fire.
Three hundred and eighty shells an hour, thirteen hours Bombardment.
Scale.

The U.S. Navy's plan of attack on Fort Anderson for February 18, 1865, outlining the warships' line of fire on the powerful earthen defenses. According to this chart, the gunboats unleashed 4,940 shot and shell during a reported thirteen hour bombardment, though the Confederate estimate of the number of incoming navy shells was much lower. Note the detailed profile for the navy's mock monitor, *Old Bogey,* used against Fort Anderson late on the night of February 18.   *Courtesy of Jim Pleasants*

sels moved into line splendidly and poured broadsides into the enemy, the enemy replied," observed Stephen C. Bartlett, a surgeon on board the *Lenapee.* "After we got our position we anchored, continued firing." For ten hours the Union warships maintained an intense and accurate bombardment.[26]

Stephen Bartlett scurried to the hurricane deck near the pilot house on the *Lenapee* to get a better view of "all that [was] going on." The ship's captain, Lt. Cmdr. John S. Barnes, ordered Dr. Bartlett to his station below deck to prepare for receiving wounded sailors. Anxious to watch the unfolding battle, however, Bartlett persuaded his superior officer to allow him to remain topside "until blood was shed." He assured Captain Barnes that he "had his instruments ready for the bloody work and [himself] prepared to amputate limbs with neatness and dispatch." As no sailors were wounded on the *Lenapee* during the day's fight, Bartlett's scalpels did not see any action, thus allowing the surgeon to remain on deck for the duration of the fierce bombardment. "The sight was most magnificent," Bartlett exclaimed. "The [enemy] are determined to sink us or blow us up but we give them broadside after broadside."[27]

> *The artillery duel between the warships and the fort impressed observers on both sides.*

The artillery duel between the warships and the fort impressed observers on both sides. As the din of battle grew louder and louder, one Union tar confessed that he found the bombardment both grand and terrible. "The screaming of the shells, loud roar of the artillery, flashing of the guns [and] bursting of the shells was a sight well worth seeing," he exclaimed. A Confederate soldier confessed to a somewhat different reaction from his vantage point inside the fort. "The shelling of the fort from the gunboats, made the place anything but comfortable," he admitted. Another gray-clad soldier, Lt. William Calder of the 1st Battalion North Carolina Heavy Artillery, recalled that the warships' "fire was tremendous and the fall and bursting of shells was almost continuous." The *Lenapee* alone unleashed four hunderd 100-pounder Parrott shells on the fort. During her four-hour bombardment of Fort Anderson beginning at noon on February 18, the *Shawmut*

The double-ender gunboat *Lenapee* (shown here) and other Union warships "moved into line splendidly and poured broadsides into the enemy, the enemy replied," observed Stephen C. Bartlett of the unfolding naval battle at Fort Anderson on February 18, 1865. *N.C. Division of Archives and History.*

Wilmington artist Chuck Leise depicted this scene of Fort Anderson's Battery B under attack by the U.S. Navy on February 18, 1865. Sixteen warships unleashed thousands of projectiles on the Brunswick bastion during a continuous ten -hour bombardment. *Author's Collection*

let loose thirty-six 100-pounder Parrott shells, twenty-nine 30-pounder Parrotts, and two 9-inch cannonballs. By General Hagood's count, the Federal warships fired a combined total of 2,723 projectiles on the fort—about one every ten seconds—nearly every shell striking the earthworks or landing inside.[28]

Under the circumstances it was surprising that the Confederates suffered as few casualties as they did (about fifteen men). Admiral Porter's terrific naval cannonade inflicted most of the Confederate losses. Artillerymen manning the guns on Battery B near the river bore the brunt of the naval fire, and the wounded. Lieutenant Robert Bond Vause of Company A, 40th North Carolina Regiment, was killed instantly by concussion, "without a single fragment having struck him," when a navy shell burst above his head. Lieutenant John Z. Davis of the same unit was mortally wounded in the stomach by another shell, and died the following day in a hospital at Wilmington. Private William T. Mason of Company I, 40th North Carolina, also suffered a mortal wound, and passed away in a Wilmington hospital on February 21. Private Lawrence Lancaster of the 40th's Company F, lost an arm to the surgeon's sharp saw after being hit by a projectile fragment. One Tarheel ordnance officer, Lt. Eugene S. Martin, recalled a close brush with death when an 11-inch Dahlgren shell exploded and ricocheted off the brick face of St. Philip's Church. A large iron chunk of the cannonball flew between him and Col. John J. Hedrick as they stood upon the fort's parapet. The whizzing fragment cut Hedrick's sword from his side, leaving the colonel shaken but unhurt. General Hagood reported casualties in the infantry on the right of the line "did not exceed half a dozen" during the day's fight.[29]

The Confederate artillerymen responded as best they could to the rain of heavy missiles on the fort. Their sight obscured by smoke hovering around the cannon muzzles and rising geysers of sand from exploding shells on the ramparts,

An out-of-focus but previously unpublished photograph of Lt. Robert Bond Vause of Company A, 40th North Carolina Regiment, who was killed instantly by concussion when a Union navy shell exploded directly over his head at Fort Anderson on February 18, 1865. *Courtesy of John Vause*

the Southerners' countershots began to fly more and more erratically toward the warships on the river. "The rebel garrison fired but wildly, striking all about [the ships], and even passing over and falling astern," claimed one Union observer. "With [the gunboats'] bursting shells in and about the fort, and throwing up such volumes of sand with every discharge, the rebels were driven to cover."[30]

Contrary to Union accounts, Johnson Hagood claimed that "not a man of the garrison" sought refuge in the underground bombproofs, but stood resolutely by their guns, even as the fort around them suffered terribly from the bombardment. According to all accounts, the earthworks did indeed suffer considerable damage. "The fort was knocked out of all shape," remarked one North Carolinian. Bursting shells pitted the ramparts, and eroded sections of the parapet and traverses. The south face of Battery B, the angle of the fort closest to the river, experienced the most disfigurement. "The wooden revetment had gradually given way; the epaulment was much torn up; in fact, in one place breached nearly to the level of the gun platform; and the traverses knocked out of shape," exclaimed General Hagood. Despite the heavy physical damage inflicted on the works, however, the defenses remained strong and none of the fort's cannon were dismounted, much less put out of action. The continued presence of the big guns, moreover, provided a strong incentive for the Federals to shy away from attempting a frontal assault against the defenses.[31]

Confederate artillerists who braved the intense naval bombardment to man their weapons answered the flotilla with only occasional shots, firing just fifty-three shot and shell all day. General Hagood admitted that his guns fired "at intervals, more in defiance than in hopes of injuring the enemy." His antiquated ordnance was all but worthless against the Federal gunboats, as once again they assumed positions beyond the range of the Confederates' mostly 6.4-inch, 32-pounder smoothbore pieces. Even the two rifled 32-pounders proved ineffective against the enemy warships. Unfortunately for the Confederates, their best hope of inflicting damage on Porter's flotilla, the deadly 12-pounder Whitworth, had expended its ammunition dur-

Pvt. Thomas H. Sutton of Company C, 40th North Carolina Regiment, seen here in a previously unpublished postwar image, recalled that Confederate cannonballs fired at the Union monitor *Montauk* during the Battle of Fort Anderson, "would strike and bounce off like cherries from a boy's pop gun against a solid wall of masonry." *Courtesy of Anna Sherman*

ing the previous day's battle. The gun had been taken north to lower Town Creek bridge to await a supply of ammunition ordered from Wilmington. Only thirty rounds could be obtained, however, and they arrived too late for the Whitworth to be of any further benefit to the Confederates at Fort Anderson.[32]

A few Confederate 32-pound balls, however, did manage to find their mark. The *Mackinaw* took a port-side hit below the water line, and was fortunate she did not suffer more serious damage to her hull. Despite their modest success in battling the unarmored steam vessels, however, the Southern artillerymen quickly learned that their ordnance was powerless to injure the monitor. Fort Anderson's guns fired twenty 6.4-inch solid iron balls at the *Montauk*— almost half of their shots unleashed during the day's fight. At least seven of them struck the "iron monster's" turret, but each ricocheted harmlessly into the murky waters of the Cape Fear River. One Confederate gunner, Pvt. Thomas H. Sutton of Company C, 40th North Carolina, left an apt description of Southern efforts to damage the ironclad and its crew. The projectiles, he later recalled, "would strike and bounce off like cherries from a boy's pop gun against a solid wall of masonry."[33]

General Hoke watched and listened to the Fort Anderson fight from his headquarters at Sugar Loaf directly across the Cape Fear River. In an effort to divert some of the Union naval fire aimed at the fort, Hoke ordered a battery of light artillery to shell the enemy's gunboats. Stationed on the summit of the fifty-foot high Sugar Loaf sand dune, Capt. Thomas Southerland's Wilmington Horse Artillery began hurling its shells about 2:00 p.m. in the direction of Porter's warships. The firing had little effect other than to distract the *Nyack*, which turned her attention against the pesky field artillery for about two hours. The *Nyack*'s fire quickly ended Hoke's retaliatory attack.

Despite Hoke's best intentions to aid Hagood, the Confederate guns at Fort Anderson had largely fallen silent by 3:00 p.m. Occasional shots rang out from the fort, but they were intended primarily to let the Federals know that the Confederates still held the fort. As the sun began to dip behind the backdrop of long leaf pine trees at Fort Anderson, Admiral Porter ordered his warships to slacken their fire, as well. The Federal gunners had performed a good day's work. Lieutenant Commander William G. Temple of the *Pontoosuc* deemed the battle "a nice little fight. The rebs stand up to their work manfully," he respectfully acknowledged, "but we are too much for them, and hope to drive them out of Wilmington before many days."[34]

General Cox had a similar intention in mind as he and his flanking force of Casement's and Sterl's brigades reached the headwaters of Orton Pond at twilight. General Adelbert Ames' division had not yet arrived, but about 175 dismounted Confederate cavalrymen, wielding carbines and British Enfield rifle-muskets, were there to dispute Cox's effort to march around the lake. Commanding the gray-uniformed horsemen was Col. Thomas J. Lipscomb of the 2nd South Carolina Cavalry, who had just that day reinforced General Hagood with an additional fifty veterans of the saddle. Lipscomb's cavalry had dug rifle pits on the north side of Moore's Creek, a shallow stream bordered by a wide marsh that fed into Orton Pond. These pits overlooked a narrow causeway that crossed the creek.[35]

Colonel Lipscomb dutifully sent word to General Hagood of the enemy's movement as soon as the Federals appeared in his front. For some inexplicable reason Hagood—who earlier had expressed anxiety about his exposed right flank and had sent cavalrymen there to warn him of any danger from that direction—now displayed little concern at all. Upon receiving Lipscomb's alarm, Hagood dispatched but a single howitzer and crew of Company B (Badham's

General Cox's flanking force reached the western end of Orton Pond about sunset on February 18, quickly brushed aside Confederate cavalry defending the point, and positioned itself to attack the rear of Fort Anderson the following morning. *Author's Collection*

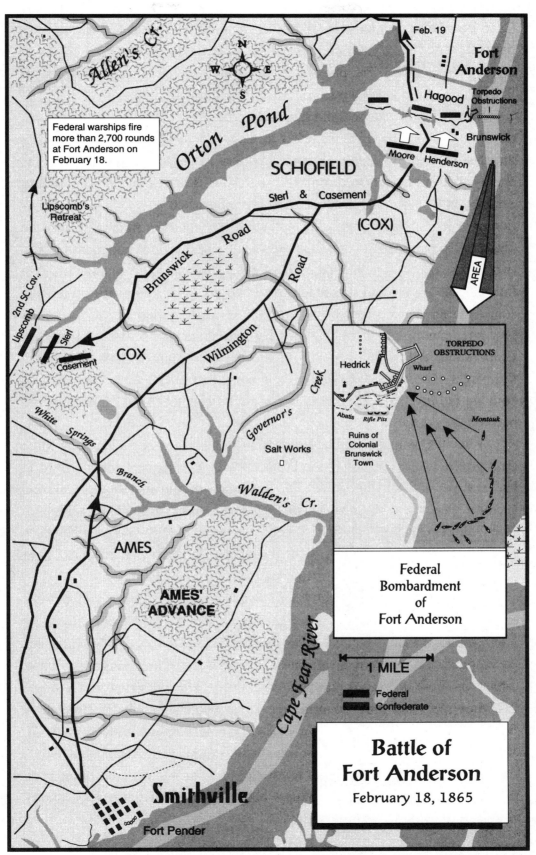

Federal warships fire more than 2,700 rounds at Fort Anderson on February 18.

SCHOFIELD

Sterl & Casement

(COX)

Lipscomb's Retreat

2nd SC Cav.

Lipscomb

Sterl

Casement

COX

Brunswick Road

Wilmington Road

Governor's Creek

Salt Works

White Springs

Branch

Walden's Cr.

AMES

AMES' ADVANCE

Smithville

Fort Pender

Cape Fear River

Allen's Cr.

Orton Pond

Feb. 19

Fort Anderson

Hagood

Torpedo Obstructions

Brunswick

Moore   Henderson

AREA

Federal Bombardment of Fort Anderson

Hedrick

TORPEDO OBSTRUCTIONS

Wharf

Road Way

Abatis   Rifle Pits

Montauk

Ruins of Colonial Brunswick Town

|←——— 1 MILE ———→|

Federal
Confederate

Battle of Fort Anderson
February 18, 1865

Mark A. Moore

Battery), 3rd Battalion North Carolina Light Artillery, commanded by Lt. John M. Jones, to reinforce the Palmetto State troopers. Perhaps Hagood was misinformed as to the size of Cox's force, or was foolishly optimistic that his fellow South Carolinians could turn back the Federals. Whatever his thoughts, 175 horse soldiers armed with carbines and a smattering of Enfield rifle-miskets, backed up with but a single field piece, were hardly sufficient to stop any sizeable force let alone the 3,000 infantrymen that Cox intended to throw around Hagood's flank. In the end Hagood's weak effort proved moot, for the lone cannon did not reach Lipscomb in time to help him anyway.[36]

Unwilling to let the encroaching darkness hamper his movement to outflank Fort

---

The aggressive Jacob Cox pushed his command around Orton Pond.

Anderson, the aggressive Jacob Cox pushed his command around Orton Pond. Once in position he deployed Companies A, D, E and I of the 104th Ohio Infantry as skirmishers with orders to advance through the marsh. Lieutenant Horace Reed of Company I led his party along the banks of the causeway under sharp fire from the dismounted Confederate cavalrymen. "The swamp was in many places impassable, so we made slow and tedious progress in crossing, but we did it," noted an Ohio infantryman. Braving the enemy's carbine fire, one by one the Union soldiers reached the north side of the creek.

When he felt he had amassed a large enough force, Lieutenant Reed ordered a bayonet charge against the dug-in Southerners. The Ohioans responded with enthusiasm, driving

Lipscomb's horsemen out of their works and putting them to flight. "[The Rebels] gave us a warm reception as we floundered thru the black mud to the higher ground, when they took to their heels and lit out," remarked Nelson A. Pinney of the 104th Ohio. Lieutenant Reed, however, who had so well organized the crossing and assault, collapsed with wounds in both legs while another Ohioan, Pvt. John Hammond of the 104th's Company E, was killed. Private Adam Weaver survived the attack, but only because a family member saved him. A bullet had ripped into Weaver's left thigh, knocking him face down into the cold creek. Adam's cousin, Rhody, saw him drop, and fearing he would soon drown, dodged zinging minie balls to pull him to safety.[37]

The Federals suffered fewer than ten casualties during the half-hour engagement. Confederate losses are unknown, but were probably minimal as well. The Federals gave chase to the Confederate cavalry for a mile or more but managed to capture only a handful of isolated stragglers. With the crossing secured, Cox advanced Sterl's and Casement's brigades around the pond. The depth of the pursuit seemed to indicate to General Cox that there was no organized Confederate resistance behind the enemy's right flank. The rear of Fort Anderson beckoned.[38]

It had been a long and fatiguing day for the men of General Ames' division. They had been awakened before midnight by Schofield's sudden order to move from Federal Point to the west side of the Cape Fear River to reinforce Cox. The transfer of 4,000 soldiers across the harbor took all night, and it was not until early on the morning of the 18th before all of the men had disembarked at Smithville. There Ames' infantrymen joined Cox's supply wagons for the trip to the headwaters of Orton Pond. But the wagon train, which Ames' division was supposed to accompany, was not yet ready to roll, leaving the sleepy and disgruntled soldiers marking time waiting for the convoy to get started.

The situation appeared more favorable when the wagons and foot soldiers finally began to advance, but before long the column became lost in the backwoods. Disgusted with their train-sitting chore, Ames' infantry trudged on, leaving the wagons to find their own way. With the aid of one of General Cox's staff officers and a black guide, whom Cox had sent to find the missing force, Ames finally reached Orton Pond at 5:45 p. m. But the general's woes were far from over.

In the encroaching darkness Ames' vanguard, Company D of the 117th New York Infantry, stumbled into Cox's rear guard, and a firefight threatened to erupt before the two forces discovered that they had mistaken each other for the enemy. It was a close call, recorded an Ohio soldier: "While waiting for the remainder of the boys to cross the corduroy causeway across the swamp, we noticed quite a force coming up the road to the south, which we took to be the rebels, and formed a skirmish line to receive them. They also formed in a line of battle, and sending their skirmishers forward, advanced to the attack, and we would probably have been hotly engaged in a few minutes had not some of our men discovered that they bore the Union flag and wore the blue. A small detail carried to

Brevet Major General Adelbert Ames was ordered to bring his division of troops from Federal Point to Brunswick County to support General Cox's movement around Orton Pond on Fort Anderson's west flank. *Author's Collection*

them tidings of who we were." Having averted the near disaster, Ames' troops joined Cox's on the north side of Moore's Creek. Collapsing in the woods, the Union troops were soon fast asleep.[39]

Rumors about the situation at Fort Anderson swept through the streets of Wilmington on Saturday, February 18. The citizens had heard the booming of cannon throughout the day, as they had all afternoon the previous day. Their attempts to learn of the fort's fate, however, were ignored by the military authorities, who refused to reveal any details about the on-going battle. Given their indignant opinion of the absent General Braxton Bragg, many of Wilmington's citizens believed that the fall of Fort Anderson to the Yankees was a done deal. "The people in Wilmington seem to think the enemy can take possession whenever they are ready," claimed one resident.[40]

Other civilians, tried to allay those fears. "Rumors were abroad this morning that Fort Anderson had fallen or been evacuated," reported James Fulton, editor of the *Wilmington Daily Journal.* "This is not so, for the enemy kept up their firing nearly all night, which would not have been the case had the Fort fallen into their hands." Like most civilians, Fulton knew little about the battle raging downriver, and could offer his readers no details. But in Saturday evening's paper he offered what he did know. "The Fort is where it always was—on Brunswick Point, and the Confederate flag still floats over it," he reported. Even as the rumble of heavy artillery pealed through his office, Fulton implored his audience "not to place any confidence in street rumors. . .or the tales of (so-called) reliable gentlemen." As long as Fort Anderson remained in Confederate hands, so would Wilmington.[41]

As Wilmingtonians fretted over the fate of their beloved city and its defenders, the Confederate garrison at Fort Anderson prepared for an expected enemy assault at dawn. Work details repaired damage to the earthworks and placed additional obstructions at the sally port near the river, in case Union infantry or a naval landing party tried to attack by way of the shoreline. All the while, Porter's gunboats lobbed shells into Fort Anderson to demoralize its defenders and disrupt their effort to rest. After sunset, the gunboats slackened their fire to one shot every five minutes. At 11:00 p.m., the Federals further reduced their shelling to one shot every thirty minutes, but from 2:00 a.m. until sunrise on the February 19, the warships increased their fire to six rounds an hour. Lieutenant William Calder tried to rest alongside his Confederate comrades in their makeshift shanties along the earthen lines, "but it was in fear and trembling lest a shell might penetrate it and blow it to atoms. I don't think I ever passed such a night," Calder complained, "but I got a little troubled sleep between the shells."[42]

While the gunboats threw missiles into the fort, Admiral Porter attempted an ingenious plan that, if successful, would enable his flotilla to move closer to the fort in the morning—or even capture it outright. Some days earlier, the resourceful Lt. Cmdr. William B. Cushing had suggested using a Quaker monitor against Fort Anderson. Cushing hoped that the Confederates would mistake the fake ironclad for the *Montauk* and be tricked into detonating their torpedoes in an effort to sink her. With the threat of buoyant mines removed, the navy would be able to press its attack with greater vigor from closer range. Admiral Porter liked the idea, having employed a sham gunboat (the "Black Terror") himself during the Vicksburg campaign in late February 1863. Porter approved Cushing's scheme.

Using an old scow, barrel staves and canvas, carpenters threw together the Quaker monitor near Smithville. When completed, "it was not possible to distinguish between it and the real one at 200 yards distance," Cushing bragged. The imitation ironclad was promptly dubbed *Old Bogey* and *Albemarle No.2*, in commemoration of the Confederate ram *Albemarle* the intrepid lieutenant commander had sunk at Plymouth, North Carolina four months earlier. On the evening of February 13, Cushing had *Old Bogey* towed upriver for her maiden voyage against Fort Anderson, but foul weather forced him to postpone the launch. The determined naval officer tried again to deploy the dummy craft late on the night of February 15, but again his efforts were thwarted by bad weather.[43]

Finally, under a starry sky on February 18, Cushing had the unmanned mock monitor moved upstream at 9:45 and set adrift about 200 yards from the mouth of Fort Anderson's obstructions. To make sure *Old Bogey* went "straight up" the river with the flood tide, Cushing weighted the front end of the vessel much heavier than the back end. As the lieutenant commander hoped, the river's flow, which ran about five knots, carried the counterfeit craft through the fort's barricade. She eventually came to rest on the east side of the river above Sugar Loaf.[44]

The "plot worked most successfully," reported a war correspondent on assignment with the U.S. Navy. "The craft sailed past the fort in utter contempt of the guns and the torpedoes which were exploded all about her." Referring to it as "an amusing affair altogether," Admiral Porter declared that "the Rebs blew up all their submarine batteries on her without effect as she drew so little water." One of Porter's subordinates, Lt. Cmdr. William G. Temple of the *Pontoosuc*, echoed the admiral's assertion, claiming that "Johnny Reb let off his torpedoes without effect on it." Lieutenant Commander Cushing alleged even more impressive results, maintaining that the ruse—for which he could claim much of the credit—prompted the terrified Confederates to retreat from Fort Anderson. Cushing even boasted as much to President Lincoln and Secretary of the Navy Gideon Welles when he met with them in Washington on February 22, just four days after the incident. Cushing had been sent north by Admiral Porter to have a torpedo fitted to a boat to combat the Confederate ram *Stonewall*, reportedly en route to Wilmington from France. According to Secretary Welles, "the President was cheerful and laughed heartily over Cushing's account of the dumb monitor which he sent past Fort Anderson, causing the Rebels to evacuate without waiting to spike their guns."[45]

Despite Cushing's vainglorious assertion, his ploy did not provoke the Confederate evacuation of Fort Anderson. General Hagood did not even mention the affair in his postwar memoir, which is the best extant Southern account of the battle. It is unlikely that the Confederates exploded more than a few torpedoes, if any, in an effort to sink the sham monitor. Unknown to Cushing and Porter, Hagood and his garrison had suspected for several days that the Federals were constructing one or more mock ironclads to send against the fort. "We imagine they intend floating them by some dark night & make us explode our electric torpedoes under them and then send the real monitor by," predicted Lt. William Calder. "Or they may send them by all at once," he continued, "and run the risk of our blowing up the right one. But 'forewarned is forearmed,' you know, and we will try and thwart our cute Yankee friends and render this Yankee trick abortive." The Confederates knew the Quaker monitor was but a "cute Yankee" trick and thus paid it little heed. They could not afford to invest much attention in Cushing's ruse because they were much too worried about the all too real threat approaching their rear.[46]

A crude contemporary engraving of Lt. Cmdr. William B. Cushing's fake monitor *Old Bogey*, which he sent against Fort Anderson late on the night of February 18, 1865. The Confederate evacuation of the fort before dawn the following morning led Cushing to believe that his ruse had precipitated the retreat–a myth that was perpetuated by newspaper reporters. *Harper's Weekly*

By late Saturday night, February 18, Johnson Hagood realized he was in serious trouble. The defeat of Colonel Lipscomb's cavalry at Orton Pond and information gleaned from both prisoners and deserters convinced the Palmetto State general that a superior enemy force was in position to strike the rear of Fort Anderson. In all probability the attack would come at first light, and Hagood's tired and overwhelmed troops would be no match against a determined assault force three times larger than their own. Hagood expressed his concerns in a late-night telegraphic message to General Hoke at Sugar Loaf.

Hoke immediately dispatched a staff officer from Sugar Loaf to confer with Hagood at Fort Anderson. "General Hoke invited [my] expression. . .upon the propriety of withdrawing from the Fort Anderson lines," Hagood recalled. It was given by telegraph." The report received by Hoke about 1:00 a.m. was dismally bleak. In addition to Cox's menacing flanking force, Hagood detailed for his superior that he had, "a very much larger force than my own 600 yards in my front, in full view by daylight, and with the fleet to co-operate." Hagood's conclusion was brief and blunt: "When the force on my right rear moves, I must abandon this position, or sacrifice my command." Although Hagood closed his telegram by suggesting to Hoke that if his right was reinforced "the case presented would be different," both officers knew that there was no substantial Confederate force in the area able to help.

Lieutenant William Calder, adjutant of the 1st North Carolina Battalion Heavy Artillery, wrote to his mother in Wilmington that the Confederates knew of the Federals' plan to send a bogus monitor past Fort Anderson in hopes that the garrison would be tricked into detonating its torpedoes in the Cape Fear River. *Courtesy of Robert Calder*

Despite Hagood's presence at the scene and carefully detailed situation report, Hoke procrastinated. "What do you think best?" he asked Hagood, fully aware that the evacuation meant that Sugar Loaf would have to be abandoned as well. The South Carolinian quickly wired another telegram reiterating his prior assessment—only this time in a more urgent tone: "I think this place ought to be evacuated and the movement commenced in half an hour." By now it was 2:05 a.m., February 19.[47]

Even though Robert Hoke knew a hopeless situation when he saw one, he did not reply to Hagood's second message for almost three-quarters of an hour. It is likely that Hoke dallied while contemplating General Bragg's message of February 8, which expressed the department commander's caution that "except in an extreme case, involving the safety of the command, [Fort Anderson] will not be abandoned." The Brunswick bastion had been held until the last moment, but now Hoke realized there was nothing to be gained by losing both the fort and its garrison. With time ticking away, Hoke knew he had to act. Finally, at 2:48 a.m., Hoke wired Hagood his approval to evacuate Anderson, along with orders for him to take up a new line of defense at Town Creek, a little more than seven miles to the north. When Hoke's instructions finally arrived, Hagood ordered an immediate withdrawal. "Having but a very small force there to oppose [the enemy], with the fort torn up so badly, and no heavy guns on our left [near the river], and a flanking force on the right with nothing to oppose them," explained a member of the Confederate garrison, "we could do nothing but fall back."

Field artillery, ordnance wagons and ambulances comprised the first wave of withdrawals from the fort. Quartermaster and commissary wagons, which during the battle had been moved to Allen's Creek, were also sent toward Town Creek. Most of the garrison held on until just before dawn, when it hurriedly evacuated the fort it had so well defended. Hagood's pickets remained at their posts so as not to alert the enemy as to what was transpiring. The pace of the retreat, which began in an organized manner, became so hurried in the end that the dead were reportedly left behind, laid out in the ruins of St. Philip's Church. The fort's heavy artillery and ammunition were also abandoned in the haste to evacuate the position, and the cannon were left unspiked. As Hagood explained it: "No effort was made to blow up the magazine of the

fort or to destroy its armament because of the shortness of the time till daylight after the evacuation order was received." General Hoke, Hagood added, "had requested by telegraph that the magazine should not be exploded before 6:30 a.m." While it is possible that the celerity of the withdrawal prevented the spiking of the guns, Hagood's statements can also be interpreted as a rebuke of Hoke for delaying the order to evacuate the fort.

Hagood sent word to Colonel Lipscomb, whose troopers had been keeping an eye on Cox's Federals at Orton Pond, to retire to upper Town Creek bridge. Lipscomb's cavalry was to act as a flanking force for the main column, which was marching to lower Town Creek bridge. It was almost dawn before Hagood directed his pickets to withdraw from their positions in front of the fort.[48]

The Federals attacked Fort Anderson at first light, almost simultaneously with the retreat of

Portions of General Hagood's army withdrew from Fort Anderson up this road, the Orton Plantation causeway, before dawn on February 19, 1865. The stately brick columns were erected many years after the war, probably in the 1930s. *Brunswick Town State Historic Site*

Hagood's pickets. Union pickets had heard noises coming from inside the work throughout the early morning hours and suspected an evacuation was underway. Major Frank Wilcox of the 63rd Indiana Infantry led the first wave of attackers—skirmishers from Thomas Henderson's brigade. Henderson's men fired a volley in the direction of the battered sand walls and advanced on the run, scaling the fort's ramparts without opposition. By then Fort Anderson was all but deserted. "They smelled the rat and evackuated the fort before we got there," recorded a disappointed Union soldier, perhaps anxious for a little scrap with the defiant Southerners.[49]

Although no serious fighting occurred, the Federal skirmishers entered the work in time to capture forty or fifty soldiers of Hagood's rear guard. Among the captives were Lt. Macon Bonner and at least five of his comrades from Company B, 40th North Carolina. Other companies from the same regiment lost a similar number of men to the Union vanguard. Private Chistopher C. Barnes of the 40th North Carolina's Company B was wounded during the rapid retreat, perhaps by a rifle-musket shot from the advancing Federals, but managed to escape along with the main Confederate force heading northward toward Town Creek. His less fortunate comrades captured on Fort

---

The Federals attacked Fort Anderson at first light, almost simultaneously with the retreat of Hagood's pickets.

Anderson's skirmish line would spend the winter and spring in Northern prisoner-of-war camps.[50]

Skirmishers in the brigade of Col. Thomas J. Henderson, seen here in a postwar photograph, were the first Union troops to enter Fort Anderson in the wake of the Confederate withdrawal. *U.S. Army Military History Institute*

Upon entering Fort Anderson, the Federals also took possession of a garrison flag, "which was rolled up and evidently had fallen off a wagon during the hasty withdrawal." A soldier of Company A, 140th Indiana Infantry, found the standard lying crumpled on the ground, and turned it over to the regiment's commander, Col. Thomas J. Brady. Four weeks later, on March 17, Colonel Brady presented Anderson's banner to Governor Oliver P. Morton of Indiana at a ceremony in front of the National Hotel in Washington. To show his appreciation for the governor's loyal support of his Republican administration, President Lincoln also appeared at the gathering, rather than attend a stage performance at the Campbell Hospital near the Soldiers' Home as he had planned. Lincoln took time to review the 140th Indiana and make a few remarks to the excited crowd of people who had come for the presentation of the "captured flag of Fort Anderson." But as one Union soldier later scoffed: "it was not captured, it was found." Ironically, Lincoln's attendance at the flag ceremony may have ultimately cost him his life. March 17 was the same day that John Wilkes Booth had planned to kidnap the president as he made his way to the Campbell Hospital. With his abduction scheme foiled by Lincoln's change of schedule, the deranged Booth altered his plan for Lincoln's fate.[51]

The Hoosier volley delivered before storming Fort Anderson's deserted walls prompted Col. Orlando Moore to quickly form his own brigade into line of battle with fixed bayonets and order it foward toward the fort. Apparently oblivious to the Confederate withdrawal, Colonel Moore thought the small arms fire indicated a battle at hand. The only troops his brigade encountered, however, were some of Maj. Frank Wilcox's Indiana skirmishers spreading word of the fort's abandonment. Members of the 111th Ohio Infantry claimed the honor of being the first unit of Moore's brigade to raise regimental col-

ors on the enemy ramparts. As soon as he reached the fort, Colonel Moore grabbed the colors of the 26th Kentucky Infantry and planted them on the parapet of Battery B as a signal to the navy that Fort Anderson had been captured. In light of the fort's earlier occupation by Thomas Henderson's regiments, one Illinois soldier considered Colonel Moore's actions a "complete farce." "As soon as he had discovered the situation of affairs, [Colonel Moore] ordered his brigade into line and actually went through the form of making an assault upon the abandoned rebel works. . . he may have succeeded in dividing the honors, but the fact remains that Major Wilcox and his skirmishers [of Henderson's brigade] were the first to take possession of the fort."[52]

Admiral Porter was unaware of the situation inside Fort Anderson when, about 6:15 a.m., the monitor *Montauk* and the gunboat *Sassacus* renewed the bombardment. Later there was some speculation that the naval gunners, having spotted the flag of the 26th Kentucky on the fort, mistook it for a defiant Confederate standard, and opened fire. Fortunately for the fort's new occupants, the Union vessels had unleashed at most half a dozen shots when the navy learned of the fort's fall. Even so, the thun-

Union infantry stormed over Fort Anderson's earthen wall about sunrise on February 19, 1865, and reportedly (though it appears unlikely) found dead Confederate soldiers laid out inside the ruins of St. Philip's Church. *Author's Collection*

derous report of the warships' big guns and the bursting of shells in and around the earthworks caused panic among the occupying blue-clad troops. Terrified soldiers dashed to the river, and waved their kepis, coats, and flags, and blew bugles as a signal to the navy that they now possessed the fort. Colonel Orlando Moore rode his charger to the riverbank and "shook out a square yard of white canvas dog tent and waved toward the fleet as a flag of truce." Elias Smith, who accompanied the army as a correspondent with the *New York Tribune*, flapped his cloak as a signal to the warships to hold their fire.[53]

Porter's ships got the message, though the sailors later admitted their delight at having accepted the fort's surrender from the U.S. Army—perhaps the only such incident of the war. The *Montauk*, lying closest to the fort, hoisted a white flag to halt the bombardment, a display that prompted gunboat commanders to order their men to climb the rigging of their ships to cheer the victory. "The enemy had skedaddled during the night," recorded a Union naval diarist. "They did not like those IX & XI-inch rotten shots I guess," he continued, referring to the giant shells the flotilla had peppered the fort with for two days.[54]

For David D. Porter, however, Fort Anderson's fall was not enough. The admiral wanted his fleet to receive due credit for its capture, and would later falsely claim that the navy had occupied the fort for half an hour before the army arrived. An Illinois soldier recalled that he saw Porter come ashore with a marine escort about 7:30 a.m. on February 19, and then proclaim "formal possession of the fort in the name of the United States Navy."[55]

While Porter may have been more concerned about Fort Anderson's fall for political reasons, General Schofield was satisfied with the victory for itself. The army commander immediately notified General Terry of the fort's capture, though Terry may already have known. The general and his troops on Federal Point probably heard the celebration going on across the river, and Terry's pickets had recently reported that the Confederates had withdrawn from Sugar Loaf. Following Hagood's lead, Hoke's troops also slipped away during the early morning hours of February 19. They were marching up the east bank of the river toward Wilmington when the Federals discovered their empty earthworks. Upon receiving the intelligence, Terry moved his force into the abandoned Confederate trenches, where it briefly rested before beginning its pursuit.[56]

While Terry's men on Federal Point may have been aware of Fort Anderson's change of ownership, word had not traveled to the Union left flank on the mainland. For several hours Jacob Cox and Adelbert Ames did not know of Hagood's hasty retreat. Early morning found

> *. . . the Union sailors later admitted their delight at having accepted the fort's surrender from the U.S. Army . . .*

them still waiting for the supply wagons from Smithville to reach Orton Pond. Cox, whose men were hungry, thought it prudent to wait for the supply train and feed his troops before pressing the attack on Fort Anderson. After having spent most of the previous day in disarray on the backroads of Brunswick County, the wagon train had turned around and gone back to Smithville to reform and begin its journey anew. The wagons finally reached the front and Cox's famished infantry about 10:00 a.m. on February 19.[57]

Anxious to make the attack, Cox advanced within the hour toward what he believed was Hagood's exposed right flank with Ames' division, the first unit to be resupplied by the late arriving wagons. The Ohioan left behind Sterl's and Casement's brigades to draw rations and follow. Cox and Ames had advanced about halfway to Fort Anderson when they met Capt. William A. Lord of General Schofield's staff, who had been sent to inform them of the Brunswick bastion's capture. Ames proceeded on to the fort with his division, which was transferred back to Terry's command across the river later that afternoon, while Cox waited for his two brigades to catch up with him. Mid-afternoon found Colonels Sterl and Casement reunited with Henderson and Moore on the Wilmington Road about two miles north of Fort Anderson. The advance of Henderson and Moore from the direction of the fort had been delayed until engineers repaired the bridge across Orton canal, which had been damaged by the Confederates during their evacuation. As soon as the brigades had reformed, they pushed upriver in pursuit of Hagood's retreating Confederates.[58]

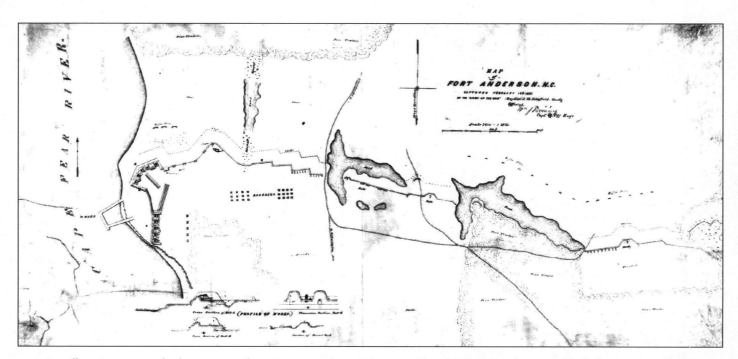

Captain William J. Twining, chief engineer in the Department of North Carolina, made this detailed map of Fort Anderson and the profiles of its artillery batteries shortly after Union forces captured the Brunswick stronghold. *Courtesy of Jim Pleasants*

THE NEW YORK HERALD.

WHOLE NO. 10,405.   NEW YORK, THURSDAY, FEBRUARY 23, 1865.   PRICE FOUR CENTS.

THE CAPTURE OF FORT ANDERSON.

Important Operations of Major General Schofield and Admiral Porter—Another Step Towards the Investment of Richmond.

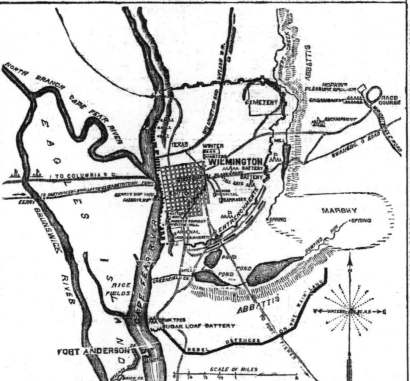

The Union victory at Fort Anderson was considered so important in the North that the *New York Herald* of February 23, 1865, devoted its entire front page to news reports about the battle, including a fanciful map.

Author's Collection

Chapter 4

The Aftermath

Today, looking due southward from the top of Fort Anderson's Battery A, the rear of Battery B and auxillary earthworks are easily discernible. During the battle, all of the trees in the background would have been cut down to give Confederate artillerists clear fields of fire downriver. *Courtesy of Jerry Netherland*

As Jacob Cox was advancing his men, Admiral Porter met General Schofield onshore to inspect Fort Anderson. The massive earthen fort and its collateral defenses awed the officers. "They are very strong and rendered almost inaccessible by swamps," Schofield reported. Other Union observers were equally as impressed with the place. "[Fort Anderson] is a work of great extent, covering nearly as much ground as that of Fort Fisher; it is a work of immense strength," noted war correspondent Elias Smith. In addition to the strong earthworks, the fort also ceded the victorious Northerners several fine prizes, including ten pieces of heavy ordnance, a considerable quantity of ammunition, some prisoners and the garrison flag.[1]

For the Union, the capture of Fort Anderson—like that of Fort Fisher—attested to the efficiency and cooperation of its army and navy. The strategy behind the combined operation was well-planned and the tactics executed with precision, determination and harmony. As one astute reporter noted: Fort Anderson was yet "another splendid trophy to the combined valor

of the Army and Navy." Despite Admiral Porter's initial misgivings about General Schofield's command decisions, the two leaders communicated well enough to ensure the capture of Wilmington's last major defensive work. "Thus, one by one, do the strongholds of the Rebellion yield to the restless energy of our Union forces," boasted one reporter. "Fort Anderson—which almost as securely and defiantly as Fort Fisher held the mouth of this last breathing-lung of Rebel supply—is now in our possession, without the loss of a boat and scarcely loss of a man." Another Federal observed somewhat more succinctly: "Fort Anderson is ours. The river is ours. Wilmington is virtually ours."[2]

Fort Anderson's importance to Confederate Wilmington was evident in Braxton Bragg's message to Generals Hoke and Hagood on February 8 not to abandon their positions unless absolutely necessary. By the early morning hours of February 19, however, Hagood convinced Hoke that Fort Anderson's evacuation was, indeed, necessary to save his command from capture by Cox's flanking force, which, after turning Orton

"Fort Anderson is ours. The river is ours. Wilmington is virtually ours."

Pond, threatened to gain the fort's rear and cut off the garrison. The Palmetto State general committed a fatal error in not adequately supporting his weak right flank, though it should be pointed out that his garrison force was too small to sufficiently cover Fort Anderson's mile-long sand wall and the extreme right beyond Orton Pond.

Safe behind his earthworks after having repulsed the determined Union attack against Sugar Loaf on February 11, General Hoke might have considered dispatching another brigade for Fort Anderson's protection. At the time, Hoke commanded three brigades of about 4,500 troops strongly entrenched along the Sugar Loaf line. Sending a brigade of 1,500 infantrymen to Fort Anderson would have cut Hoke's force by one third, but it would have also significantly augmented Hagood's far weaker force of 2,300 soldiers attempting to defend more ground in Brunswick County than Hoke's men on Federal Point. Surely, Hoke knew that the Federals transferred a division of men to the mainland on February 16 to attack Fort Anderson. In less than a day, Confederate troops could have been safely transported from Sugar Loaf to Fort Anderson or to the dock at Orton Plantation, from where they could have marched the last mile-and-a-half to the fort.

For General Hoke, the decision not to reinforce Fort Anderson and the subsequent loss of the Brunswick fortress had ramifications beyond his expectations. Since Fort Anderson and the defensive position at Sugar Loaf mutually supported one another, the loss of the former meant

that the latter was no longer tenable. Thus Anderson's evacuation precipitated the abandonment of Sugar Loaf, as Hoke realized that the U.S. Navy would soon control the Cape Fear River north of his position, leaving his force exposed to enfilading fire and possible capture. He had no choice but to withdraw toward Wilmington.[3]

The Federals were not about to let the Confederates get comfortable behind fresh defensive positions. With Fort Anderson and Sugar Loaf now securely in their possession, Cox's and Terry's infantry advanced rapidly up both sides of the river, while Porter's flotilla ascended the Cape Fear River in support. Minesweepers cleared the river of torpedoes off Fort Anderson, allowing the gunboats to steam methodically upstream, keeping pace with Schofield's forces.

On the afternoon of February 20, General Terry's two brigades of U.S. Colored Troops clashed with Hoke's entrenched Confederates at Forks Road three miles south of Wilmington. The clattering rifle-musket volleys and booming field artillery at Forks Road was punctuated by the thunderous reports of heavy cannon to the west, as Porter's gunboats dueled with Confederate shore batteries along the Cape Fear River. The din of battle could also be heard on the river's opposite shore, where General Cox's division engaged Hagood's troops from Fort Anderson in their new defensive position at lower Town Creek bridge.

Having failed to spring his trap at Fort Anderson, Cox was determined to try again. Using an abandoned rice barge, the Ohio general crossed three of his four brigades over Town Creek and into Hagood's rear. The movement took Hagood completely by surprise, and forced the South Carolinian to again flee his position. Still, Cox's aggressive force bagged 375 men and offi-

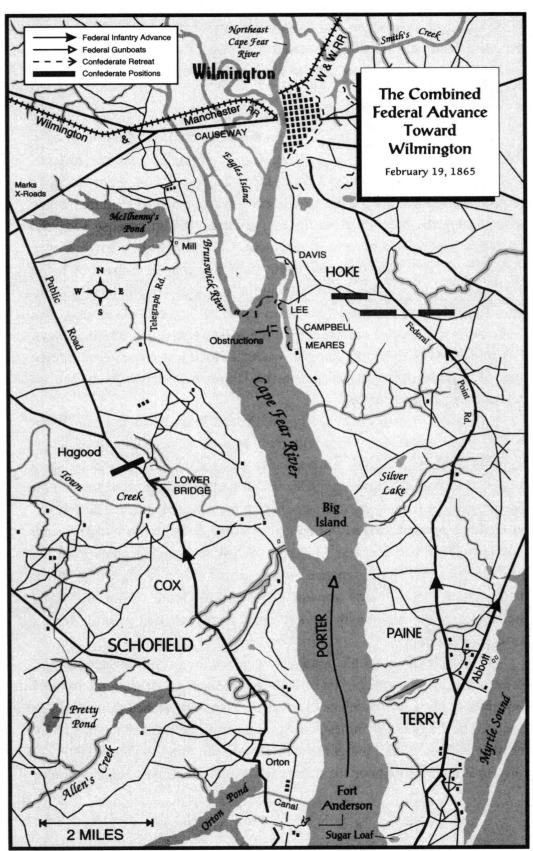

Federal Infantry Advance
Federal Gunboats
Confederate Retreat
Confederate Positions

Northeast
Cape Fear
River

Smith's Creek

W & W RR

Wilmington

Wilmington & Manchester RR

CAUSEWAY

**The Combined
Federal Advance
Toward
Wilmington**

February 19, 1865

Marks
X-Roads

McIlhenny's
Pond

Mill

Eagles Island

Brunswick River

DAVIS

HOKE

Public Road

Telegraph Rd.

LEE

CAMPBELL

MEARES

Obstructions

Federal

Cape Fear River

Point Rd.

Hagood

Town Creek

LOWER
BRIDGE

Silver
Lake

Big
Island

COX

PORTER

PAINE

SCHOFIELD

Abbott

Pretty
Pond

TERRY

Myrtle Sound

Allen's Creek

Orton

Orton Pond

Canal

**Fort
Anderson**

Sugar Loaf

2 MILES

Mark A. Moore

cers of the Confederate rear guard, two pieces of field artillery and several battle flags. Hagood's main force managed to elude capture, however, and retreated to Wilmington. Cox followed in close pursuit, deploying his infantry and artillery on the banks of the Brunswick River, two miles west of Wilmington, by mid-afternoon on February 21. A brief duel between Cox's artillery and Hagood's field pieces positioned in downtown Wilmington, demonstrated that the Federals were capable of putting shells into the city. Meanwhile, a force of Cox's skirmishers pushed within rifle-musket range of the city's waterfront.

General Bragg finally returned from Virginia on February 21. With the Federals now within

---

"Our success virtually put an end to the rebellion...."

---

striking distance of Wilmington, Bragg ordered an evacuation of the city. Before sunrise the following morning, Hoke's and Hagood's demoralized Confederate troops packed up their belongings and headed northward toward Kinston. Following behind the retreating Southerners, Union forces occupied Wilmington early that same morning, February 22.

After the loss of Wilmington, the Confederate high command consolidated scattered armies in North Carolina for a showdown with Sherman's rapidly advancing army. General Joseph E. Johnston was assigned to command those forces, including the remanants of the Army of Tennessee, Lt. Gen. William J. Hardee's army retreating from South Carolina and General Bragg's army from Wilmington.

General Grant had foreseen that threat to Sherman when he sent Schofield's corps to North Carolina to help capture Wilmington and reinforce Terry's and Sherman's armies. The city's fall gave the Federals control of the Cape Fear River, which they soon ascended to Fayetteville, 100 miles to the northwest. Union soldiers from Wilmington were waiting for General Sherman when his army reached Fayetteville on March 11, and supplies soon followed. This enabled Sherman's army to continue its advance toward Goldsboro without detouring to the seacoast.

The Confederates struck Sherman at Bentonville, where for three days, March 19-21, Johnston and Sherman traded blows in what turned out to be the largest land battle of the Carolina's Campaign. After suffering heavy casualties which they could ill afford, the Confederates withdrew. Johnston's retreat allowed Sherman to regroup and push on to Goldsboro. Generals Schofield, Cox and Terry linked forces with Sherman at that juncture, bolstering the blue-clad legions to 88,000 troops, enough men to challenge any Confederate threat. Sherman's army was also positioned near the North Carolina seacoast, which Admiral Porter's navy now controlled, and it had railroads for supplies and reinforcements from Wilmington and New Bern. Well armed, well fed and in fighting shape, Sherman's army was poised to attack Robert E. Lee in Virginia.

With Grant renewing the offensive on March 29, and his rear vulnerable to attack from Sherman in North Carolina, Lee believed he had little choice but to abandon his position along the Petersburg-Richmond line. As he had predicted, if Wilmington fell the Army of Northern Virginia must give up the Richmond-Petersburg defenses. No longer able to supply his depleted and beleaguered troops via the Wilmington & Weldon Railroad, and threatened by two far superior armies, Lee had to move. Grant followed on Lee's heels, battling and racing him to Appomattox Courthouse, where Lee surrendered on April 9, 1865.

Without renewing hostilities, Joseph E. Johnston, along with the remnants of Bragg's army, capitulated to Sherman at Durham Station, North Carolina, on April 26. The four-year war was over, and the fall of Wilmington played a key role in its outcome. The Union victory not only severed the Confederacy's last lifeline, but it guaranteed the success of Sherman's Carolinas Campaign. Admiral Porter put it more eloquently when he wrote, "The result of our capture [of Fort Anderson and the other Cape Fear forts] was felt throughout rebeldom. Our success virtually put an end to the rebellion, for nothing could come to the rebels from that direction. It enabled us also to communicate with General Sherman who was closing in upon Wilmington and he could push right on without stopping to hunt up for provisions which were now supplied him by the Wilmington railroad."[4]

The Battle of Fort Anderson witnessed more human activity at the site than any other time in its history. The fort's 2,300 Confederate defenders confronted 10,000 Union ground forces (once Ames' division joined the fight) and hundreds of sailors and marines on board vessels on the Cape Fear River. After the Confederate evacuation of the Brunswick defenses, however, only a small unit of U.S. troops remained at the fort for security purposes.

One responsibility of the occupation forces was dealing with displaced persons. In the closing days of the war, 6,000 to 8,000 refugees made their way to the Lower Cape Fear, having been sent there by General Sherman, whose army they had attached themselves to as it advanced through the Carolinas. Wilmington, however, could not accommodate the thousands of mostly black men, women and children, who were desperate for food, clothing and shelter. Facing a crisis, the local U.S. military authorities placed the refugees on deserted lands and plantations throughout the region. Fort Anderson soon became a temporary home to hundreds of disaffected people, who lived in the deserted Confederate barracks. By late April 1865, however, most of them had been resettled elsewhere, and Brunswick was again abandoned, as it had been in the days following the American Revolution. Nevertheless, a few of the refugees may have squatted at Brunswick. Many years after the war, Jeffrey Lawrence, a former house slave of a prominent Charleston family, was discovered living in a small cabin in the woods near St. Philip's Church. An enchanting storyteller, Lawrence quickly became a favorite with the children of Orton's then landlord, Col. Kenneth M. Murchison.[5]

United States forces officially occupied Fort Anderson for only a brief stint, but the earthen bastion remained a curiosity for military personnel stationed in the Lower Cape Fear. They roamed about the site marvelling at the strong earthworks and searching for souvenirs. Even though the battle there was over, the fort still posed considerable danger. For two young black sailors, it proved to be a deadly place.

On March 7, 1866, Thomas Coates and Stephen Bruce of the U.S. Revenue Cutter *Northerner* anchored off Fort Anderson, went ashore for "a pleasure excursion." On exploring the deserted fort, the men wandered into one of Battery B's underground shelters. Once inside the dark chasm, one of the seamen lit a match and then discarded it on the floor. Coates and Bruce did not know that gunpowder, unused in the battle a year earlier, lay scattered about the chamber. A heavy blast suddenly rocked the fort, as the powder magazine exploded and then collapsed. The detonation blew one of the sailors out of the magazine's door and scorched the face of his friend.

The severely injured men were rushed for treatment to the Seaman's Home in Wilmington, where, on March 9, Thomas Coates died. "The deceased came to his death from burns, caused by the accidental explosion of a Confederate magazine at Fort Anderson," reported the *Wilmington Daily Journal.* Coates' friend, Stephen Bruce, remained in critical condition.[6]

Perhaps the tragedy that claimed Thomas Coates' life made people wary about visiting Fort Anderson. Perhaps it was the site's isolation that kept visitors away. Whatever the reason, by all accounts Fort Anderson and the surrounding area quickly relapsed into a vegetative state. Thick undergrowth, scrub oaks, and pine trees soon covered the imposing battlements. At some point, the silent 32-pounder cannon were removed from their wooden carriages and sent to the North or broken up for scrap. After visiting the abandoned defenses, Wilmingtonian

---

Although largely deserted after 1865, Fort Anderson was not forgotten. . .

Alfred Moore Waddell waxed poetic when he observed: "since [the war] it has again relapsed into its former state, and the bastions and traverses and parapets of whilom Fort Anderson are now clad in the same exuberant robe of green with which generous nature in that clime covers every neglected spot. And so the old and the new ruin stand side by side, in mute attestation of the utter emptiness of all human ambition, while the Atlantic breeze sings gently amid the sighing pines, and the vines cling more closely to the old church wall, and the lizard basks himself where the sunlight falls on a forgotten grave."[7]

According to one observer, "everything went to pieces" after the untimely death of Brunswick's owner, Thomas C. Miller, Jr., in June 1865. Miller, whose vast Orton tract included Fort Anderson and Old Brunswick, had maintained the site in the days immediately following the war. Unable to meet the heavy financial demands of Orton after Miller passed away, however, the family lost the property. The plantation's 9,026 acres of rice fields and forest of longleaf pine and hard wood trees, the mansion and its numerous outbuildings, as well as the colonial ruins of Brunswick and Fort Anderson were advertised for sale at public auction on August 22, 1872, to satisfy creditors' claims against the Miller estate.

Four years later, a young Englishman named Currer Richardson Roundel purchased Orton. Roundel's brief tenure as Orton's landlord ended with his tragic death by suicide, prompting his heirs to dispose of the huge plantation. Two former Confederate officers, Maj. Charles M. Stedman and his brother-in-law, Capt. David M. Murchison, bought Orton in the late 1870s. About 1880, however, they sold the property to Captain Murchison's older brother, Kenneth M. Murchison. A veteran officer of the 54th North Carolina Infantry, Colonel Murchison diverted much of the fortune he had made in cotton and naval stores to revive Orton Plantation, which had fallen into considerable disrepair since the war.[8]

Although largely deserted after 1865, Fort Anderson was not forgotten, particularly by Confederate soldiers who had served there. Twenty-five years after the Battle of Fort Anderson, former gunner Barnabas Edwards of Eustis, Florida, wrote to the editor of the *Wilmington Messenger,* inquiring about his old comrades of Company C, 1st Battalion North Carolina Heavy Artillery, whom he had not seen since February 1865. "I think a reunion of the battalion would be a nice thing for us all," Edwards exclaimed. "One thing I do know, I would like to meet those old boys once more . . .espcially our beloved first captain, Alexander MacRae." While several well-attended reunions of Confederate and Union veterans of the

Wilmington Campaign were held in the city and at Fort Fisher in the late nineteenth and early twentieth centuries, such a gathering at Fort Anderson does not appear to have occurred.[9]

Still, the old fort was visited from time to time. In early September 1880, Wilmington residents James G. Burr, William Waters, Wilkes Morris and the Rev. Alfred A. Watson of St. James Episcopal Church journeyed to Old Brunswick to examine St. Philip's Church. For years the men had heard tell that Union soldiers, in their search for booty at Fort Anderson, had broken into the tombs in St. Philip's graveyard, and removed the church's cornerstone to steal its contents. The gentlemen hoped their visit to Brunswick Town and Fort Anderson would reveal the truth about the Yankees' alleged disrespectful behavior.

Much to their dismay, Burr, Waters, Morris and Watson found the church's cornerstone missing and many of the nearby marble tombstones broken, defaced and scattered about. "It was very evident from the appearance of the [church] wall that some parties had been searching for the cornerstone long before our visit, for a hole of considerable size had been made in the northeastern portion of the wall," observed James G. Burr. "We became satisfied that. . .the cornerstone of the old church was lost to us forever, and this became confirmed the day after our return to Wilmington." In a conversation with a member of Burr's search party, Wilmington photographer C.M. Van Orsdell claimed that during the 1865 Union occupation of the city, a Federal officer showed him an old newspaper, silver and copper coins, and a cross contained in a metallic box reportedly taken from the cornerstone of St. Philip's Church.[10]

Interest in Old Brunswick increased dramatically after the formation of the Cape Fear Chapter of the North Carolina Society of the Colonial Dames of America in 1896. Three years later, the organization made its first trek to St. Philip's Church to pay homage to the Cape

Fear's colonial and Revolutionary War heroes and heroines and their deeds. Each May for the next five decades, the Cape Fear Dames made their "pilgrimages of patriotism" to Brunswick. In 1902, the state chapter erected an inscribed marble plaque in St. Philip's edifice to commemorate Maurice Moore, who is considered Brunswick Town's principal founder.[11]

The society occasionally paid tribute to local Confederate soldiers of the "late unpleasantness." In the spring of 1900 the Cape Fear Dames invited Eugene S. Martin, former lieutenant in Company A, 1st Battalion North Carolina Heavy Artillery, to give an address on the Battle of Fort Anderson. A large crowd of lavishly attired ladies and gentlemen gathered at St. Philip's Church on May 1 to hear Lieutenant Martin's presentation:

> We stand on hallowed ground. . .hallowed by the many memories that cluster around this historic spot. . .Of those brave [Southern] men and the storm of war that raged around this old town I am here to speak today. . . .It is well that you have this commemorative service. It is well to recall the character of our forefathers, to brush from their tombs the dust that has gathered upon them in the years gone by. It is honorable that those who bear the names keep the graves and boast the blood of these patriotic men should tenderly revere their memories and dwell with pride upon their exalted virtues. Thus gazing long and intently upon them we may pass into the likeness of the departed, may emulate their virtues and partake of their immortality.[12]

One of the earliest and more active presidents of the Cape Fear Dames was Luola Murchison Sprunt, daughter of Orton's Col. Kenneth M. Murchison and wife of James Sprunt, former purser's clerk on several blockade runners during the Civil War, postwar cotton magnate, philanthropist and Cape Fear historian. After the war, James and his father established Alexander Sprunt & Son, which became the largest U.S. cotton exporting firm in the world. Upon the death of his father-in-law in 1904, James Sprunt purchased Orton and presented it to his wife. Mrs. Sprunt spent much of her final days restor-

Wilmington photographer Eric Norden captured lavishly attired ladies of the Cape Fear Colonial Dames and their gentlemen escorts during their annual "pilgrimage of patriotism" to St. Philip's Church at Old Brunswick, circa 1900. *Courtesy of Steve McAllister*

ing and adding onto the Orton mansion and planting a beautiful garden around the estate. She also led a crusade to survey and mark statewide historic sites, including Brunswick Town and Russellborough.[13]

After Mrs. Sprunt's death in 1916 and that of her husband eight years later, ownership of Orton (and thus Fort Anderson), passed to son James Laurence Sprunt. He attempted to make Orton more accessible to visitors, in part by making improvements to the old Wilmington and Telegraph Roads leading to the city. Up to that time, Orton was accessible primarily by river. Eventually North Carolina's Department of Transportation assumed the maintenance of Brunswick County's roads, including the one that passed near Orton, which was paved and designated N.C. Highway 133. As a result, more and more visitors flocked to the Lower Cape

Fear's only surviving colonial plantation and to view its magnificent gardens.[14]

After World War II, the U.S. Army announced plans to establish a huge ordnance depot in Brunswick County on property adjacent to Orton. Fearful that Old Brunswick and Fort Anderson would fall within the army terminal's highly sensitive easements and thus be declared off limits to all visitation, Cape Fear historian E. Lawrence Lee implored the Sprunt family to work out a mutual agreement with the State of North Carolina that would allow Brunswick to be open to the public. Lee's entreaty and the Sprunts' deep appreciation for the history of the Lower Cape Fear, convinced authorities that closure of the site would be a great loss to the people of the region, as well as the state. Consequently, on December 22, 1952, the Sprunt family sold a 114.5 acre tract containing most of Brunswick Town and the main portion of Fort Anderson to North Carolina for the grand total of $1.00. Four months later the Episcopal Diocese of East Carolina transferred ownership of St. Philip's Church and its surrounding five-acre plot to the state for the same amount. In 1955, North Carolina's Division of Historic Sites in the Department of Archives and History established the Brunswick Town State Historic Site.[15]

The state's plan for development of Brunswick Town as a state historic park met with some objections from the U.S. Army. Although the government was not unsympathetic with North Carolina's desire to develop Brunswick, they were concerned about civilian activity, security and safety in the backyard of the top secret ordnance stores base. After considerable negotiating, however, the parties reached an agreement in 1957 that provided for an historic buffer zone within the easements of the army's Military Ocean Terminal, Sunny Point. The government exercises restrictive control over building, development and visitation at the historic park. It can close, and has closed, Brunswick to visitation at times of a national military emergency, such as during the Persian Gulf War in 1991.

With an agreement between North Carolina and the U.S. government finally in hand, Lawrence Lee began systematically locating Brunswick Town's buildings and streets in June 1958. For years Lee had painstakingly researched colonial Cape Fear deeds and studied C.J. Sauthier's 1769 *Plan of the Town and Port of Brunswick*. Lee also cleared some of the jungle of undergrowth that had consumed the site, enabling him to pinpoint more than thirty of Old Brunswick's ruins.[16]

In early August 1958, Lee stepped aside when the state assigned professional archaeologist Stanley A. South to the Brunswick Town project. Although a trained prehistory archaeologist who had been working at North Carolina's Town Creek Indian Mound, South quickly learned the art of historical archaeology at Brunswick. For almost eleven years, South and his loyal foreman Charlie Smith, along with their crew of laborers and volunteers, discovered some sixty archaeological features, and unearthed the foundations of twenty-three structures, as well as hundreds of colonial and Civil War artifacts. Extensive excavations were performed at pri-

Confederate engineers built Fort Anderson over the ruins of some of Brunswick Town's colonial structures, including the Newman-Taylor house seen here after being excavated by archaeologists in 1961. *Courtesy of Thomas E. Beaman, Jr.*

Dr. Stanley A. South, head archaeologist at Brunswick Town from 1958 to 1968, carefully whisks away dirt and debris from the remains of a brick floor in the Nathaniel Moore house. *Brunswick Town State Historic Site*

vate colonial dwellings, the courthouse, the public house and tailor shop, the royal governor's palace and one Confederate barrack. Trowels also scraped the soil inside St. Philip's Church. Visitors to the site observed and sometimes participated in the ongoing excavations. Buttons, bottles, bullets and other artifacts uncovered in and around the features were displayed in cases erected adjacent to the ruins. South later recalled finding an unexploded 15-inch cannonball weighing 300 pounds that had been fired by the monitor *Montauk* during the Battle of Fort Anderson. He disarmed the shell by unscrewing the brass watercap fuze and pouring out the still dry and explosive gunpowder. The buzz of activity at Brunswick revealed a living, breathing historical site.[17]

In 1961, the state appropriated $6,000 exclusively for the recovery of Fort Anderson. Of that amount, $5,000 was targeted for clearing the canopy and carpet of vines, bushes and trees

that covered the ramparts, and the $1,000 balance was slated for erecting trail-side exhibits. South employed a crew of about ten men, that began bush-axing Batteries A and B and the western wall of the fort up to St. Philip's Church. A huge accidental brush fire one afternoon cleared the fort's ramparts in a matter of hours, whereas it would have taken South and his men weeks to defoliate the same amount of ground. In September 1961, South reported that 12,000 people had visited the "double site" in the first nine months of that year alone.

As interest in and visitation to Fort Anderson and Brunswick Town increased during the 1960s, North Carolina's new Department of Cultural Resources, the Brunswick County Historical Society, the Friends of Brunswick Town, and other state and local historical and preservation groups donated additional time and money to the site. In 1964, the North Carolina Division of the United Daughters of the

Confederacy financed the construction of two pedestrian bridges, which connected some of Fort Anderson's lofty riverside earthworks. Although dismantled for safety reasons twenty years later, the wooden walkways enabled history buffs to traipse the summit of the mounds without having to scale the steep embankments.[18]

In 1967, a much needed visitor center to display and interpret the colonial and Civil War artifacts unearthed at Brunswick opened to the public. Today, the center is undergoing a major face lift, with plans for both expansion and newly designed exhibits. A reproduced slide presentation will offer visitors a brief overview of the site's rich history. Since opening more than thirty years ago, the center's most captivating display is a beautiful impressionistic hand-cut

Venetian tile mosaic of Brunswick Town's defense against the 1748 Spanish attack on the seaport. The large artwork, which greets visitors as they enter the building, was crafted by the late Claude Howell, one of the Lower Cape Fear's most gifted artists, with assistance from Catherine Henricksen. On display below Howell's mosaic is an iron cannon pulled from the Cape Fear River in 1986, which is believed to be from the *Fortuna*, one of two Spanish sloops that attacked Brunswick.

Unfortunately, the grand opening of the Brunswick visitor center in 1967 was soon followed by a change in state policy toward historic sites. Strapped by budgetary woes, the Department of Cultural Resources halted all archaeological projects at state-owned parks in 1968, including Brunswick Town and Fort

The Brunswick Town State Historic Site visitor center opened its doors in April 1967. On display inside are hundreds of colonial and Civil War artifacts uncovered on site. A portion of Fort Anderson's earthen wall is visible in the background on the righthand side of the building. *Brunswick Town State Historic Site*

The centerpiece of the Brunswick Town State Historic Site visitor center is this hand-cut Venetian tile mosaic depicting Brunswick's defense against the 1748 Spanish attack, and an iron cannon believed to be from the Spanish sloop *Fortuna* that sank in the Cape Fear River during the battle. *Brunswick Town State Historic Site*

Anderson. The focus at the sites shifted from historical interpretation to maintenance. With archaeology no longer a priority in North Carolina, Stanley South accepted a position as state archaeologist with the South Carolina Institure of Archaeology and Anthropology.

North Carolina's Department of Cultural Resources replaced South with William Faulk, whose primary responsibilities were keeping Brunswick cleared, clean and safe for visitors. Ironically, the site's alligators—perhaps descendants of the reptiles that had occupied Brunswick when Lt. Thomas Rowland began building Fort St. Philip in 1862—seemingly received as much publicity as the site itself. Faulk even began adding alligators to Brunswick pond in the summer of 1969, that is, until the reptiles became too abundant for safe keeping. Despite the lack of state funds, Faulk supervised the construction of a nature trail at Brunswick and assembled a research library in the visitor center.

While the state has yet to revive its archaeological efforts at Brunswick, tourists still view the colonial ruins excavated by Stanley South and his staff. Also visible are such features as

A walkway on Battery B is seen in this February 1965 snapshot. *Courtesy of D. "Mule" Skinner*

On October 13, 1964, the North Carolina Division of the United Daughters of the Confederacy presented two pedestrian bridges at Fort Anderson to the Department of Archives and History. Confederate reenactors (far left) participated in the ceremony. *Brunswick County Historical Society Newsletter*

wells and rubble piles of brick and ballast stone, which mark the location of additional colonial and Confederate dwellings and various domestic outbuildings, including kitchens and smokehouses.

In more recent years the Brunswick Town State Historic Site staff, led by James A. Bartley since 1987, has developed new ways to interpret the history of the area. Bartley directed construction of outdoor illustrated trail markers that inform visitors of Fort Anderson's and Brunswick's past. Living history demonstrations and teacher workshops on early American life are offered during Heritage Days each autumn. To mark the February anniversary of the Battle of Fort Anderson, the site sponsors an annual Civil War reenactment and living history program. Authentically uniformed and armed reenactors offer guided tours through their encampment, perform the manual-of-arms and marching drills, and fire rifle-muskets and light artillery. Civil War historians give presentations on the fort's fascinating story and, together with staff members, offer walking tours around the earthen defenses.[19]

These programs, together with Fort Anderson's history and excellent state of preservation, are drawing serious attention from Civil War scholars and buffs alike. The massive earthworks reflect a project of impressive engineering skill, ingenuity and labor. Today, the battlements loom as large and as strong as they did when attacked by Union forces 134 years ago.

> *The massive Confederate earthworks reflect a project of impressive engineering skill, ingenuity and labor.*

Visitors to the Brunswick Town State Historic Site totalled about 50,000 in 1998 alone, and that number is steadily increasing due in large part to interest in Fort Anderson. After touring the site in October 1993, Edwin C. Bearss, then chief historian of the U.S. National Park Service, declared that Fort Anderson was the finest and most well preserved Confederate coastal fortification he had seen.

The Brunswick bastion is finally shedding its undeserved reputation as the Lower Cape Fear's *other Confederate fort.*

The Brunswick Town State Historic Site commemorates the February anniversary of the Battle of Fort Anderson with a Civil War encampment and living history demonstrations. *Brunswick Town State Historic Site.*

Confederate Garrison at Fort St. Philip-Fort Anderson

Capt. Calvin Barnes' Company Unattached North Carolina Artillery
later designated 2nd Company H, 40th Regiment North Carolina Troops,
served at Fort St. Philip ca. April 1862-April 1863

Capt. Alexander MacRae's Company Heavy Artillery
later designated Company C, 1st Battaltion North Carolina Heavy Artillery,
served at Fort St. Philip ca. April 10-May 17, 1862

Capt. George Tait's Company North Carolina Volunteers
later designated 2nd Company K (Bladen Artillery Guards), 40th Regiment North Carolina Troops,
mustered in at Fort St. Philip on May 15, 1862 and remained there through August 1862

1st Battalion North Carolina Heavy Artillery
Company D, Capt. James L. McCormic, served at Fort Anderson ca. February-April, 1864

10th Battalion North Carolina Heavy Artillery
Company A, Capt. Hammet J. Harris
served at Fort Anderson ca. July-November 24, 1864
Company B (Black River Tigers), Capt. Henry M. Barnes
dispatched temporarily to Fort. St. Philip, ca. September-October 1862,
during Wilmington's yellow fever epidemic

36th Regiment North Carolina Troops (2nd North Carolina Artillery)
Company E (Columbus Artillery), Capt. Nathan L. Williamson
served at Fort St. Philip ca. July-August 1862
Company H (Clarendon Artillery), Capt. Daniel Patterson
served at Fort St. Philip-Fort Anderson ca. May 10, 1862-early 1864

40th Regiment North Carolina Troops (3rd North Carolina Artillery)
Company A (Lenoir Braves), Capt. Ancram W. Ezzell
served at Fort Anderson October 29, 1864-February 19, 1865
Company C (Bridger's Artillery), Capt. John E. Leggett
served at Fort St. Philip-Fort Anderson ca. April 1862-November 1863

Order of Battle

Battle of Fort Anderson, February 17-19, 1865

**Confederate States Army, Department of North Carolina, Third Military District,
Fort Anderson, Brig. Gen. Johnson Hagood, commanding**

Hagood's Brigade, Col. Charles H. Simonton, field commander
7th Battalion South Carolina Infantry, Lt. Col. James H. Rion
11th South Carolina Infantry, Col. F. Hay Gantt
21st South Carolina Infantry (remnants), Col. Robert F. Graham
25th South Carolina Infantry (remnants), Col. Charles H. Simonton
27th South Carolina Infantry, Capt. Allston

Artillery
3rd Battalion North Carolina Light Artillery
Company B, Capt. William Badham, Jr.
Capt. Abner A. Moseley's Company (Sampson Artillery)

Hedrick's Brigade, Col. John J. Hedrick
1st Battalion North Carolina Heavy Artillery
Company A, Capt. Robert G. Rankin
Company B, Capt. John W. Taylor
Company C, Capt. William H. Brown
Company D (remnants), Lt. John T. Rankin
Taylor's Battery, Lt. Col. John Douglas Taylor
36th Regiment North Carolina Troops (2nd North Carolina Artillery)
remnants
40th Regiment North Carolina Troops (3rd North Carolina Artillery), Maj. William Holland
Company A, Capt. Ancram W. Ezzell
Company B, Lt. Macon Bonner
Company C, Capt. John E. Leggett
Company F, Capt. John Robertson
2nd Company H, Capt. Calvin Barnes
Company I, Capt. Charles C. Whitehurst
71st Regiment North Carolina Troops (2nd North Carolina Junior Reserves)
Company B
Capt. W.J. McDougald's Unattached Company North Carolina Troops
Coast Guard Company (unattached)

Cavalry
2nd South Carolina Cavalry (detachment), Col. Thomas J. Lipscomb

United States Army, Department of North Carolina, Wilmington Expeditionary Force, Maj. Gen. John M. Schofield, commanding

XXIII Army Corps, Maj. Gen. Jacob D. Cox, field commander
Second Division
Second Brigade, Col. Orlando Moore
107th Illinois Infantry, Maj. Thomas J. Milholland
80th Indiana Infantry, Lt. Col. Alfred D. Owen
26th Kentucky Infantry (100 men from First Brigade)
23rd Michigan Infantry, Col. Oliver L. Spaulding
111th Ohio Infantry, Lt. Col. Issac R. Sherwood
118th Ohio Infantry, Lt. Col. Edgar Sowers

Third Division
First Brigade, Col. Oscar W. Sterl
12th Kentucky Infantry, Lt. Col. Laurence Rousseau
16th Kentucky Infantry, Lt. Col. John S. White
100th Ohio Infantry, Capt. Frank Rundell
104th Ohio Infantry, Lt. Col. William J. Jordan
8th Tennessee Infantry, Capt. James W. Berry

Second Brigade, Col. John S. Casement
65th Illinois Infantry, Maj. George H. Kennedy
65th Indiana Infantry, Lt. Col. John W. Hammond
103rd Ohio Infantry, Capt. Henry S. Pickands
177th Ohio Infantry, Col. Arthur T. Wilcox
5th Tennessee Infantry, Lt. Col. Nathaniel Witt

Third Brigade, Col. Thomas J. Henderson
112th Illinois Infantry, Lt. Col. Emery S. Bond
63rd Indiana Infantry, Lt. Col. Daniel Morris
140th Indiana Infantry, Col. Thomas J. Brady

Artillery
1st Ohio Light Artillery
Battery D, Lt. Cecil C. Reed

Signal Corps (detachment), Lt. E.H. Russell

Terry's Provisional Corps, Maj. Gen. Alfred H. Terry
XXIV Army Corps
Second Division, Bvt. Maj. Gen. Adelbert Ames
First Brigade, Col. Rufus Daggett
3rd New York Infantry, Lt. George E. Avent
112th New York Infantry, Lt. Col. Ephraim A. Ludwick
117th New York Infantry, Capt. Edward Downer
142nd New York Infantry, Lt. Col. Albert M. Barney

Second Brigade, Col. William B. Coan
47th New York Infantry, Capt. Joseph M. McDonald
48th New York Infantry, Maj. Nere A. Elfwing
76th Pennsylvania Infantry, Maj. Charles Knerr
97th Pennsylvania Infantry, Maj. William H. Martin
203rd Pennsylvania Infantry, Capt. Heber B. Essington

Third Brigade, Col. G. Frederick Granger
13th Indiana Infantry, Lt. Col. Samuel M. Zent
9th Maine Infantry, Lt. Col. Joseph Noble
4th New Hampshire Infantry, Capt. John H. Roberts
115th New York Infantry, Lt. Col. Nathan J. Johnson
169th New York Infantry, Col. James A. Colvin

Disposition of United States Navy vessels on the Cape Fear River, North Carolina, February 15, 1865, Rear Admiral David D. Porter, commanding

Vessel	Guns	Commanding Officer
Bat	3 guns	
Berberry	4 guns	Acting Ensign Robert W. Rowntree
Chippewa	6 guns	Lt. Cmdr. Aaron Weaver
Emma	8 guns	Acting Mstr. James Hamilton
Eolus	4 guns	Acting Mstr. Edward S. Keyser
Huron	5 guns	Lt. Cmdr. Thomas O. Selfridge
Kansas	8 guns	Lt. Cmdr. Pendleton G. Watmough
Launch # 1	1 gun	
Launch # 6	1 gun	Acting Ensign C.S. Willcox
Lenapee	10 guns	Lt. Cmdr. John S. Barnes
Little Ada	2 guns	Acting Mstr. Samuel P. Crafts
Mackinaw	10 guns	Cmdr. John C. Beaumont
Malvern	12 guns	Ensign William C. Wise
Maratanza	6 guns	Lt. Cmdr. George Young
Maumee	3 guns	Lt. Cmdr. Ralph Chandler
Moccasin	3 guns	Acting Ensign James Brown
Montauk	1 guns	Lt. Cmdr. Edward E. Stone
Monticello	4 guns	Lt. Cmdr. William B. Cushing
Nansemond	3 guns	Acting Mstr. James H. Porter
Nyack	8 guns	Lt. Cmdr. L. Howard Newman
Osceola	10 guns	Cmdr. J.B.M. Clitz
Pawtuxet	10 guns	Cmdr. James H. Spotts
Pequot	8 guns	Lt. Cmdr. Daniel L. Braine
Pontoosuc	12 guns	Lt. Cmdr. William G. Temple
Republic	1 gun	Acting Ensign John W. Bennett
Sassacus	12 guns	Lt. Cmdr. John L. Davis
Seneca	5 guns	Lt. Cmdr. Montgomery Sicard
Shawmut	8 guns	Lt. Cmdr. John G. Walker
Unadilla	6 guns	Lt. Cmdr. Frank M. Ramsay
Wilderness	4 guns	Acting Mstr. Henry Arey
Yantic	5 guns	Lt. Cmdr. Thomas C. Harris

CHAPTER 1: THE DEFENSES

1. Johnson Hagood, *Memoirs of the War of Secession* (Columbia, 1910), pp. 338-339.

2. Chris E. Fonvielle, Jr., *The Wilmington Campaign: Last Rays of Departing Hope* (Campbell, 1997), chapters 1-2; See also: Chris E. Fonvielle, Jr., "The Last Rays of Departing Hope: Campaign for Wilmington and Fort Fisher," *Blue & Gray Magazine* (December 1994), pp. 11-15.

3. E. Lawrence Lee, *The Lower Cape Fear in Colonial Days* (Chapel Hill, 1971), chapters 11 and 16.

4. *Gleason's Pictorial Drawing Room Companion*, July 16, 1853; Alan D. Watson, *Wilmington: Port of North Carolina* (Columbia, 1992), pp.59-60; William Lord DeRosset, *Pictorial and Historical New Hanover County and Wilmington, North Carolina* (Wilmington, 1938), pp. 8-9.

5. "Decline of Brunswick Town," p. 30, Brunswick Town State Historic Site (Winnabow, North Carolina); Benson J. Lossing, *The Pictorial Field-Book of the Revolution*, 2 vols. (New York, 1860), vol. 2, p. 362.

6. Kate Mason Rowland, "Letters of Major Thomas Rowland, C.S.A.," *William and Mary College Quarterly Historical Magazine*, XXVI, No. 4 (April 1917), p. 230; United States War Department, *The War of the Rebellion, A Compilation of the Official Records of the Union and Confederate Armies,* 128 vols. (Washington, D.C., 1880-1901), series 1, Special Orders, No. 60, March 15, 1862, vol. 9, p. 445, hereinafter cited as *OR*. All references are to series 1 unless otherwise specified. Brigadier General Samuel Gibbs French remained in command at Wilmington until mid-July 1862, when he was promoted major general and the head of the Department of North Carolina, headquartered in Petersburg, Virginia, ibid, 11, pt. 3, p. 643.

7. Report exhibiting position of batteries and obstructions on approaches to Wilmington, January 25, 1864, *OR* 33, p. 426.

8. Rowland, "Letters of Thomas Rowland," *William and Mary Historical Magazine*, p. 230. Thomas Rowland was born in Detroit, Michigan on March 25, 1842, but grew up in Fairfax, Virginia. He entered the U.S. Military Academy at West Point, New York in July 1859, and resigned on April 26, 1861 to join the Confederate army. Papers of Thomas Rowland, Kate Mason Rowland Collection, Eleanor S. Brockenbrough Library, The Museum of the Confederacy, Richmond, Virginia.

9. Louis H. Manarin and Weymouth T. Jordan, eds., *North Carolina Troops 1861-1865: A Roster* 14 vols. (Raleigh, 1966-1998), vol. 1, pp. 2, 395 and 478-479.

10. Rowland, "Letters of Thomas Rowland," *William and Mary Historical Magazine*, pp. 231-232.

11. Rowland, "Letters of Thomas Rowland," *William and Mary Historical Magazine*, pp. 231-232; James Sprunt, *Chronicles of the Cape Fear River 1660-1916* (Wilmington, 1982), p. 333; Extracts from Note Books of Thomas Rowland, C.S.A., Kate Mason Rowland Papers, Eleanor S. Brockenbrough Library, The Museum of the Confederacy, Richmond, Virginia.

12. "There is nothing new down here only Col Lamb left us and gone to Fort Fisher and J.A. Richardson is in command here now [Fort St. Philip] and I think it is quite likely that he will soon leave here and go to Fort Fisher or to Zeek's Island," wrote Pvt. Archibald D. McEwen of the Bladen Artillery Guards (later designated 2nd Company K, 40th Regiment North Carolina Troops [3rd North Carolina Artillery]). Archibald D. McEwen to S.C. McEwen, July 8, 1862, Brunswick Town State Historic Site, Winnabow, North Carolina. See also: John A. Richardson to Zebulon B. Vance, September 19, 1862, Zebulon B. Vance Papers, North Carolina Division of Archives and History, Raleigh.

13. *Wilmington Daily Review*, June 25, 1894; *Wilmington Messenger*, June 26, 1894.

14. *Wilmington Daily Journal*, July 2, 1863.

15. Eugene S. Martin to Andrew J. Howell, November 6, 1919, Fort Anderson File, New Hanover County Public Library, Wilmington, North Carolina.

16. William C. Davis, ed., *The Confederate General*, 6 vols. (National Historical Society, 1991), vol. 1, pp. 18-19; Patricia L. Faust, ed., *Historical Times Illustrated Encyclopedia of the Civil War* (New York, 1986), p. 13; Ezra Warner, *Generals in Gray* (Baton Rouge, 1959), pp. 5-6; *Wilmington Daily Journal*, June 25, 1864.

17. "I inspected the armament of Fort Anderson. . .it consists of nine 32-pounder guns on barbette carriages, front pintle, wooden traverse circles. They are: Two rifled, unbanded; two oldest pattern of the U. S., which kind of guns condemned by U. S. inspectors previous to year 1860; and five pattern 1840. Below the fort is a work [Old Brunswick Battery] armed with one 32-pounder gun of oldest pattern (as described). The projectiles for these guns are 913 shot, 708 shell, 39 grape and 106 cannister shot, with a sufficient supply of projecting charge, making 170 rounds for each gun." Inclosure Report of H. Oladowski, February 5, 1865, *OR* 47, pt. 2, pp. 1116-1117. See also: *OR Atlas*, CXXXV-B, 4.

18. *Wilmington Journal*, May 28, 1863.

19. Whiting to Cooper, January 15, 1863, *OR* 18, pp. 829, 848.

20. William Calder to Mother, January 28, 1865, William Calder Papers, Southern Historical Collection, University of North Carolina, Chapel Hill (hereinafter cited as Calder Papers, Southern Historical Collection).

21. William Henry Tripp to Araminta Guilford Tripp, January 27, 1865, William Henry and Araminta Guilford Tripp Papers, Southern Historical Collection, University of North Carolina, Chapel Hill (hereinafter cited as Tripp Papers, Southern Historical Collection); *Wilmington Journal*, March 12 and May 28, 1863.

22. Manarin, *North Carolina Troops*, vol. 1, pp. 247, 398, 402-403 and 506.

23. Alfred Moore Waddell, *A Colonial Officer and His Times* (Raleigh, 1890), p. 214; *Wilmington Journal*, March 12, 1863.

24. Archibald D. McEwen to S.C. McEwen, July 8, 1862, Brunswick Town State Historic Site, Winnabow, North Carolina; William Calder to Mother, January 23, 1865, Calder Papers, Southern Historical Collection.

25. *Wilmington Journal*, March 12 and May 28, 1863; *Wilmington Daily Journal*, September 24, 1863.

26. Manarin, *North Carolina Troops*, vol.1, p. 500; *Wilmington Journal*, August 6, 1863; John A. Richardson to Zebulon B. Vance, Zebulon B. Vance Papers, North Carolina Division of Archives and History, Raleigh.

27. *Wilmington Daily Journal*, September 1, 1864; *Wilmington Morning Star*, September 9, 1917.

28. Stanley A. South, "A Nice Little Fight at Fort Anderson," unpublished manuscript, Brunswick Town State Historic Site, Winnabow, North Carolina.

CHAPTER 2: THE THREAT

1. Fonvielle, "Campaign for Wilmington and Fort Fisher," *Blue & Gray*, pp. 11-12. Quote is from: Gideon Welles, *Diary of Gideon Welles*, 3 volumes (Boston and New York, 1911), vol. 2, p. 146.

2. Fonvielle, "Campaign for Wilmington and Fort Fisher," *Blue & Gray*, pp. 15-19.

3. Faust, *Encyclopedia of the Civil War*, p. 594; William N. Still, Jr., "Porter Is the Best Man," *Civil War Times Illustrated* XVI (May 1977), p. 46.

4. Fonvielle, "Campaign for Wilmington and Fort Fisher," *Blue & Gray*, pp. 18-21, 48-52.

5. Fonvielle, *Last Rays of Departing Hope*, pp. 192-199.

6. Fonvielle, "Campaign for Wilmington and Fort Fisher," *Blue & Gray*, pp. 52-56.

7. General Orders No. 1, Head Qrs. Fort Anderson, January 17, 1865, copy in possession of the author; William Henry Tripp to Araminta Guilford Tripp, January 19, 1865, Tripp Papers, Southern Historical Collection; Anderson to Hébert, January 20, 1865, *OR* 46, pt. 2, p. 1117.

8. Fonvielle, *Last Rays of Departing Hope*, pp. 313-315.

9. Hébert to Anderson, January 18, 1865, *OR* 46, pt. 2, p. 1097; Hébert to Anderson, January 20, 1865, ibid, p. 1116; Anderson to Hébert, January 21, 1865, *IBID*, p. 1120; William Henry Tripp to Araminta Guilford Tripp, February 3, 1865, Tripp Papers, Southern Historical Collection; Bragg to Taylor, January 27, 1865, *OR* 46, pt. 2, p. 1154.

10. Fonvielle, "Campaign For Wilmington and Fort Fisher," *Blue & Gray*, p. 57.

11. William Henry Tripp to Araminta Guilford Tripp, January 27 and February 7, 1865, Tripp Papers, Southern Historical Collection; Diary entry of January 20, 1865, William Calder Diary, Perkins Library, Duke University, Durham, North Carolina (hereinafter cited as Calder Diary, Duke); William Calder to Mother, January 28, 1865, Southern Historical Collection.

12. William Henry Tripp to Araminta Guilford Tripp, January 29, 1865, Tripp Papers, Southern Historical Collection.

13. Letter of William Badham, Jr., William Badham Papers, East Carolina Manuscript Collection, Joyner Library, East Carolina University, Greenville, North Carolina; William Calder to Mother, January 28, 1865, Calder Papers, Southern Historical Collection.

14. William Calder to Mother, January 23, 1865, Calder Papers, Southern Historical Collection; William Henry Tripp to Araminta Guilford Tripp, January 29 and February 7, 1865, Tripp Papers, Southern Historical Collection; Zaccheus Ellis to Kate, February 4, 1875, copy in Brunswick Town State Historic Site, Winnabow, North Carolina.

15. Bragg to Hoke, January 25, 1865, *OR* 46, pt. 2, p. 1138; Hoke to Bragg, January 25, 1865, ibid, p. 1139; Anderson to Gordon, January 25, 1865, ibid, p. 1137.

16. Official records note that Pvt. Isaiah Smithwick of Company B, 40th North Carolina Regiment died of brain fever on February 7, 1865. Manarin, *North Carolina Troops*, vol. 1, p. 393. Company B's commander, Capt. William Henry Tripp, however, claimed that Private Smithwick died of pneumonia on the night of February 6. William Henry Tripp to Araminta Guilford Tripp, February 8, 1865, Tripp Papers, Southern Historical Collection. See also: William Henry Tripp to Araminta Tripp, January 29, 1865, Southern Historical Collection.

17. William Henry Tripp to Araminta Guilford Tripp, January 27, 1865, Tripp Papers, Southern Historical Collection.

18. Davis, *Confederate General*, vol. 3, pp. 48-49. Hagood; *Memoirs of the War of Secession*, pp. 11-14, 16-19.

19. Hagood, *Memoirs of the War of Secession*, pp. 334-336.

20. William Calder to Mother, January 23, 1865, Calder Papers, Southern Historical Collection.

21. Abstract log of *U.S.S. Malvern*, January 28, 1865, *Official Records of the Union and Confederate Navies in the War of the Rebellion*, 30 vols. (Washington, D.C., 1900), series 1, vol. 11, p. 740 (hereinafter cited as *ORN*); Grant to Sherman, February 1, 1865, *OR* 47, pt. 2, p. 193; Merlin E. Sumner, ed., *The Diary of Cyrus B. Comstock* (Dayton, 1987), p. 308; James L. McDonough, *Schofield: Union General in the Civil War and Reconstruction* (Tallahassee, 1972), p. 150; Grant to Schofield, February 19, 1865, *OR* 47, pt. 2, p. 492.

22. Sherman to Palmer, January 21, 1865, *OR* 47, pt. 2, p. 111; William T. Sherman, *Memoirs of W. T. Sherman (New York, 1990)*, p. 272; Sherman to Foster, January 29, 1865, *OR* 47, pt. 2, p. 163; Jacob D. Cox, *Military Reminiscences of the Civil War*, 2 vols. (New York, 1900), vol. 2, p. 395; Sherman to Grant, January 29, 1865, *OR* 47, pt. 2, pp. 155-156.

23. Cox, *Military Reminiscences*, vol. 2, p. 395; Grant to Schofield, February 19, 1865, *OR* 47, pt. 2, p. 492; Sherman to Grant, January 29, 1865, ibid, pp. 154-156; Schofield to Grant, February 15, 1865, ibid, pp. 436-437; Grant to Sherman, March 16, 1865, ibid, p. 859.

24. Porter to Welles, February 12, 1865, *ORN* 12, pp. 16-17; "David D. Porter Memoir," pp. 884-885, David D. Porter Papers, Library of Congress, Washington, D.C. (hereinafter cited as Porter Memoir, Library of Congress); Grant to Sherman, February 1, 1865, *OR* 47, pt. 2, p. 193.

25. James M. Merrill, "The Fort Fisher and Wilmington Campaign: Letters From Rear Admiral David D. Porter," *North Carolina Historical Review*, XXXV (October, 1958), p. 469 (hereinafter cited as Merrill, "Letters of Admiral David D. Porter," *NCHR*); Grant to Stanton, January 31, 1865, *OR* 47, pt. 2, p. 179; General Orders No.12, War Department, January 31, 1865, ibid, p. 179; John Y. Simon, *The Papers of Ulysses S. Grant*, 14 vols. (Carbondale, 1984), vol. 13, p. 336.

26. Ezra Warner, *Generals In Blue* (Baton Rouge, 1964), pp. 425-426; Faust, *Encyclopedia of the Civil War*, p. 661; McDonough, *Schofield*, p. 190.

27. Report of U. S. Grant, July 22, 1865, *OR* 46, pt. 1, p. 45-46; Grant to Stanton, February 4, 1865, *OR*, 46, pt. 2, p. 365; Rowena Reed, *Combined Operations in the Civil War* (Annapolis, 1978), p. 379.

28. Abstract from journal of Jacob D. Cox, February 4, 1865, *OR* 47, pt. 1, p. 927; Cox, *Military Reminiscences*, vol. 2, pp. 399-400; Jacob D. Cox, *Campaigns of the Civil War: The March to the Sea: Franklin and Nashville* (New York, 1900), p. 147.

29. Paul Murray and Stephen Russell Bartlett, Jr., eds. "The Letters of Stephen Chaulker Bartlett Aboard the *U.S.S. Lenapee*, January-August, 1865," *North Carolina Historical Review*, XXXIII (January, 1956) pp. 73, 77 (hereinafter cited as Murray and Bartlett, "Letters of Stephen C. Bartlett," *NCHR*).

30. Paul H. Silverstone, *Warships of the Civil War Navies* (Annapolis, 1989) pp. 8-9; David Herbert Donald, *Lincoln* (New York, 1995), p. 593; Barnes to Porter, January 24, 1865, *ORN* 11, p. 696.

31. Murray and Bartlett, "Letters of Stephen C. Bartlett," *NCHR*, p. 73.

32. Braine to Porter, January 22, 1865, *ORN* 11, p. 630; Hébert to Anderson, January 22, 1865, *ORN* 11, p. 807; Murray and Bartlett, "Letters of Stephen C. Bartlett," *NCHR*, p. 74.

33. Abstract log of *U.S.S. Shawmut*, February 3, 1865, *ORN* 12, pp. 36-37; Letter of William Badham, Jr., February 5, 1865, William Badham Papers, East Carolina Manuscript Collection, Joyner Library, East Carolina University, Greenville, North Carolina.

34. Manarin, *North Carolina Troops*, vol. 1, pp. 390-394; William Henry Tripp to Araminta Guilford Tripp, February 7, 1865, Tripp Papers, Southern Historical Collection.

35. *Wilmington Daily Journal*, February 7, 1865.

36. Abstract log of *U.S.S. Shawmut*, February 3, 1865, *ORN* 12, pp. 36-37; Porter to Welles, February 12, 1865, *ORN* 12, p. 17; Diary entry of February 3, 1865, Calder Diary, Duke; Hoke to Anderson, February 4, 1865, *OR* 46, pt. 2, p. 1204; *Raleigh Daily Confederate*, February 10, 1865; Unidentified Confederate soldier to Kate McGeachy, February 4, 1865, Catherine Jane Buie Papers, Perkins Library, Duke University, Durham, North Carolina; *Wilmington Daily Journal*, February 7, 1865.

37. Abstract log of *U.S.S. Shawmut*, *ORN* 12, p. 37; Abstract log of *U.S.S. Malvern*, February 10, 1865, *ORN* 12, pp. 173-174; Murray and Bartlett, "Letters of Stephen C. Bartlett," *NCHR*, pp. 72, 74.

38. Faust, *Encyclopedia of the Civil War*, p. 188; Cox, *March to the Sea*, pp. i-iii; Report of Jacob D. Cox, May 15, 1865, *OR* 47, pt. 1, p. 958.

39. *Wilmington Daily North Carolinian*, January 26, 1865.

40. Bragg to Vance, February 7, 1865, Zebulon B. Vance Papers, Division of Archives and History, Raleigh, North Carolina; Sale to Bragg, January 26, 1865, *OR* 46, pt. 2, p. 1142; Sale to Bragg, February 2, 1865, *OR* 47, pt. 2, p. 1083; Bragg to Davis, February 3, 1865, ibid, p. 1088; Bragg to Lee, February 9, 1865, ibid, p. 1138; Don C. Seitz, *Braxton Bragg: General of the Confederacy* (Columbia, 1924), p. 507.

41. *Charleston Mercury*, January 21, 1865; William Calder to Mother, February 10, 1865, Calder Papers, Southern Historical Collection.

42. *Philadelphia Inquirer*, February 21, 1865; Abstract from journal of Jacob D. Cox, February 10, 1865, *OR* 47, pt. 1, p. 927; Cox, *Military Reminiscences*, vol. 2, pp. 405-406; Schofield to Grant, February 8, 1865, *OR* 47, pt. 2, p. 356.

43. Abstract log of *U.S.S. Malvern*, February 5, 1865, *ORN* 12, p. 173; David D. Porter, *Incidents and Anecdotes of the Civil War* (New York, 1886), pp. 276-277.

44. Chris E. Fonvielle, Jr., "William B. Cushing: Commando at the Cape Fear," *Blue & Gray Magazine* (Summer 1997).

45. Abstract log of *U.S.S. Malvern*, February 8-9, 1865, *ORN* 12, p. 173.

46. According to the late Cape Fear historian James Sprunt, Cushing's second reconnaissance occurred on the night of February 17, 1865. James Sprunt, *Tales and Traditions of the Lower Cape Fear, 1661-1896* (Wilmington, 1896), pp. 46-48. Admiral Porter, on the other hand, reported that the reconnaissance took place on February 11. "Last night I sent Lieutenant Cushing up again to make a thorough reconnaissance. . .The boats had barely time to make good observations when they were hailed and then fired upon with grape and cannister from seven or eight guns, which kept up fire until they were out of sight. Fortunately we met with no loss." Report of David D. Porter, February 12, 1865, *ORN* 12, pp. 16-17. See also: Grant to Stanton, February 4, 1865, *OR* 46, pt. 2, p. 365; Report of David D. Porter, January 31, 1865, *ORN* 11, p. 721; David D. Porter, *The Naval History of the Civil War* (New York, 1886), p. 726; Porter to Comstock, February 8, 1865, Porter Papers, Library of Congress; Abstract log of *U.S.S. Malvern*, February 11, *ORN* 12, p. 174.

47. Murray and Bartlett, "Letters of Stephen C. Bartlett," *NCHR*, p. 74; William B. Cushing Journal, National Archives, Washington, D.C.; *New York Herald*, February 18, 1865; Charles F. Bahnson to George F. Bahnson, February 12, 1865, Sarah B. Chapman Collection, Advance, North Carolina; "A Reminiscence of Fort Anderson," *Wilmington Morning Star*, June 4, 1917.

48. Cushing Journal, National Archives; Abstract log of *U.S.S. Malvern*, February 11, 1865, *ORN* 12, p. 174; *New York Herald*, February 18, 1865; *New York Tribune*, February 18, 1865.

49. John Douglas Taylor, "Personal Recollections of Col. John D. Taylor, Thirty-Six North Carolina Regiment," pp. 4-5, Allan T. Strange Collection, Wilmington, North Carolina; *Wilmington Morning Star*, June 4, 1917; *New York Herald*, February 18, 1865.

50. Schofield to Porter, February 9, 1865, *OR* 47, pt. 2, p. 371; Sumner, *Diary of Cyrus Comstock*, p. 309; Cox, *Military Reminiscences*, vol. 2, p. 407.

51. Special Orders, No. 1, Department of North Carolina, Army of the Ohio, February 10, 1865, *OR* 47, pt. 2, p. 384; Schofield to Porter, February 9, 1865, ibid, p. 371; Porter Memoir, pp. 884-885, Porter Papers, Library of Congress.

52. Extracts from journal of John C. Beaumont, February 11, 1865, *ORN* 12, p. 33.

53. Murray and Bartlett, "Letters of Stephen C. Bartlett," *NCHR*, p. 75.

54. Abstract log of *U.S.S. Keystone State*, February 11, 1865, *ORN* 12, p. 38; Abstract log of *U.S.S. Shawmut*, February 11, 1865, ibid, p. 37; Abstract log of *U.S.S. Malvern*, February 11, 1865, ibid, p. 174; Charles F. Bahnson to George F. Bahnson, February 12, 1865, Chapman Collection; *New York Herald*, February 16, 1865.

55. Cox, *Military Reminiscences*, vol. 2, pp. 408-409; Confederate soldier to Kate, February 13, 1865, Brunswick Town State Historic Site, Winnabow, North Carolina.

56. Charles F. Bahnson to George F. Bahnson, February 12, 1865, Chapman Collection.

57. *Wilmington Daily Journal*, February 13, 1865; Zaccheus Ellis to Sister, February 12, 1865, Brunswick Town State Historic Site, Winnabow, North Carolina.

58. *Philadelphia Inquirer*, February 16, 1865; Abstract from journal of Jacob D. Cox, February 11, 1865, *OR* 47, pt. 1, pp. 927-928.

59. Sumner, *Diary of Cyrus Comstock*, p. 309; Cyrus B. Comstock Memorandum, February 12, 1865, *OR* 47, pt. 2, pp. 404-405; Special Orders, No.3, Headquarters Department of North Carolina, Army of the Ohio, February 12, 1865, ibid, pt. 2, pp. 403-404.

60. Schofield to Grant, February 15, 1865, *OR* 47, pt. 2, pp. 436-437; Special Orders, No.3, Headquarters Department of North Carolina, Army of the Ohio, February 12, 1865, ibid, pp. 403-404; Cyrus B. Comstock Memorandum, February 12, 1865, ibid, p. 404.

61. Porter Memoir, pp. 884-885, Porter Papers, Library of Congress.

62. Cushing Journal, National Archives.

CHAPTER 3: THE BATTLE

1. Diary entry of February 14, 1865, Oliver L. Spaulding Diary, Library of Congress, Washington, D.C.; Schofield to Commanding Officer, February 14, 1865, *OR* 47, pt. 2, p. 427.

2. Barney to Assistant Adjutant General, February 15, 1865, *OR* 47, pt. 2, p. 439; Hagood, *Memoirs of the War of Secession*, p. 335; Diary entry of February 15, 1865, Calder Diary, Duke.

3. Campbell to Dodge, February 15, 1865, *OR* 47, pt. 2, p. 438; Order of David D. Porter, February 13, 1865, *ORN* 12, p. 28; Report of Jacob D. Cox, May 15, 1865, *OR* 47, pt. 1, p. 959; Cox, *March to the Sea*, p. 149; Report of Oscar W. Sterl, April 28, 1865, *OR* 47, pt. 1, p. 965; B. F. Thompson, *History of the 112th Regiment of Illinois Volunteer Infantry in the Great War of the Rebellion, 1862-1865* (Toulan, 1885), p. 301. Official military returns report the strength of Cox's division at 4,458. Report of Jacob D. Cox, May 15, 1865, *OR* 47, pt. 1, p. 958. The author estimates that Colonel Orlando Moore's brigade contained approximately 1,500 troops. Diary entry of February 16, 1865, Spaulding Diary, Library of Congress.

4. Report of Jacob D. Cox, May 15, 1865, *OR* 47, pt. 1, p. 960; John G. Barrett, *The Civil War in North Carolina* (Chapel Hill, 1963), p. 281; W.G. Curtis, *Reminiscences of Wilmington and Southport, 1848-1900*, (Southport, 1900) p. 33; Thompson, *History of the 112th Illinois Infantry*, pp. 301-302.

5. Report of Jacob D. Cox, May 15, 1865, *OR* 47, pt. 1, p. 960; Cox, *March to the Sea*, p. 149; Report of Thomas J. Henderson, April 6, 1865, *OR* 47, pt. 1, p. 968; Report of Oscar W. Sterl, April 28, 1865, ibid, p. 965; Curtis, *Reminiscences*, p. 33; "Journal of Adam Weaver," *Wilmington Morning Star*, December 27, 1964; *New York Herald*, February 25, 1865.

6. Report of Jacob D. Cox, May 15, 1865, *OR* 47, pt. 1, p. 960; Report of Thomas J. Henderson, April 6, 1865, ibid, pp. 968-969; Cox to Campbell, February 17, 1865, ibid, pt. 2, pp. 471-472; Cox, *March to the Sea*, p. 149; McDonough, *Schofield*, p. 153.

7. *Philadelphia Inquirer*, February 24, 1865.

8. *New York Herald*, February 23, 1865; Murray and Bartlett, "The Letters of Stephen C. Bartlett," *NCHR*, p. 77; Hagood, *Memoirs of the War of Secession*, pp. 335-336; Diary entry of February 17, 1865, George Hern Diary, Private collection of Morris L. Yoder, Jr., Philadelphia, Pennsylvania; Abstract log of *U.S.S. Shawmut*, February 17, 1865, *ORN* 12, p. 37; Report of David D. Porter, February 19, 1865, ibid, pp. 33-34.

9. Report of David D. Porter, February 19, 1865, *ORN* 12, p. 33; Extracts from journal of John C. Beaumont, February 18, 1865, ibid, p. 33; Entry of February 8, Unidentified Union sailor's journal, Private collection of Tom Broadfoot, Wilmington, North Carolina; *Philadelphia Inquirer*, February 24, 1865; Report of Daniel L. Braine, February 17, 1865, *ORN* 12, p. 31; Murray and Bartlett, "Letters of Stephen C. Bartlett," *NCHR*, p. 77; *New York Tribune*, February 23, 1865; *New York Herald*, February 23, 1865; Hagood, *Memoirs of the War of Secession*, p. 336.

10. Hagood, *Memoirs of the War of Secession*, p. 333; *Philadelphia Inquirer*, February 24, 1865; Murray and Bartlett, "Letters of Stephen C. Bartlett," *NCHR*, p. 77.

11. *New York Herald*, February 25, 1865; Report of Thomas J. Henderson, April 6, 1865, *OR* 47, pt. 1, pp. 968-969; Report of Jacob D. Cox, May 15, 1865, ibid, p. 960; *Philadelphia Inquirer*, February 24, 1865.

12. Murray and Bartlett, "Letters of Stephen C. Bartlett," *NCHR*, p. 72.

13. Special Orders, No.7, Headquarters Dept. of North Carolina, Army of the Ohio, February 17, 1865, *OR* 47, pt. 2, p. 470.

14. Abstract from journal of Jacob D. Cox, February 18, 1865, *OR* 47, pt. 1, p. 929; Report of John S. Casement, April 9, 1865, ibid, p. 967; *New York Tribune*, February 23, 1865; Thompson, *History of the 112th Illinois Infantry*, pp. 302-303.

15. Hagood, *Memoirs of the War of Secession*, pp. 336-337; Diary entry of February 18, Calder Diary, Duke; Slann L.C. Simmons (ed.), "Diary of Abram W. Clement, 11th South Carolina Infantry," *South Carolina Historical Magazine*, LIX (1958), p. 79; author's interview with Stanley A. South of Columbia, South Carolina, April 19, 1998.

16. Diary entry of February 18, 1865, Saunders Richard Hornbrook Diary, Indiana Historical Society, W.H. Smith Memorial Library, Indianapolis, Indiana; Report of Thomas J. Henderson, April 6, 1865, *OR* 47, pt. 1, p. 969.

17. Report of Jacob D. Cox, May 15, 1865, *OR* 47, pt. 1, p. 960; Murray and Bartlett, "Letters of Stephen C. Bartlett," *NCHR*, p. 76; *New York Tribune*, February 18, 1865.

18. Report of Jacob D. Cox, May 15, 1865, *OR* 47, pt. 1, p. 960; Cox, *March to the Sea*, p. 149; Barrett, *The Civil War in North Carolina*, p. 282; *New York Herald*, February 25, 1865.

19. Report of Jacob D. Cox, May 15, 1865, *OR* 47, pt. 1, pp. 960-961; W. S. Thurstin, *History One Hundred and Eleventh Regiment Ohio Volunteer Infantry* (Toledo, 1894), p. 116; Issac R. Sherwood, *Memories of the War* (Toledo, 1923), p. 161; Report of Thomas J. Henderson, April 6, 1865, *OR* 47, pt. 1, p. 969; Hagood, *Memoirs of the War of Secession*, p. 336; *New York Herald*, February 25, 1865.

20. Report of Jacob D. Cox, May 15, 1865, *OR* 47, pt. 1, p. 960. Cox's flanking force was guided on its march to the western end of Orton Pond by a local black, possibly Lem Brown. Thomas Speed to parents, February 25, 1865, Thomas Speed Collection, Filson Club, Louisville, Kentucky. See also: Curtis, *Reminiscences*, p. 33. Cox's route of march was the Brunswick or British Road along the south bank of Orton Pond. *OR Atlas*, CXXXII, 1; Sprunt, *Chronicles of the Cape Fear River*, map between pp. 412-413; Hagood, *Memoirs of the War of Secession*, pp. 335 and 337.

21. Simmons, "Diary of Abram W. Clement," *South Carolina Historical Magazine*, p. 79.

22. Diary entry of February 18, 1865, Theodore J. Wagner Collection, Cape Fear Museum, Wilmington, North Carolina; *New York Tribune*, February 23, 1865; Hagood, *Memoirs of the War of Secession*, p. 336; Thomas Speed to Parents, February 25, 1865, Speed Collection, Filson Club.

23. *New York Tribune*, February 23, 1865.

24. *New York Herald*, February 25, 1865; *New York Tribune*, February 23 and 25, 1865.

25. Potter to Porter, February 18, 1865, *ORN* 12, p. 32; Diary entry of February 18, 1865, George Hern Diary, Morris L. Yoder, Jr. collection, Philadelphia.

26. Report of David D. Porter, February 19, 1865, *ORN* 12, pp. 33-34; Murray and Bartlett, "Letters of Stephen C. Bartlett," *NCHR*, p. 78.

27. Murray and Bartlett, "Letters of Stephen C. Bartlett," *NCHR*, pp. 74 and 77-78.

28. Murray and Bartlett, "Letters of Stephen C. Bartlett," *NCHR*, p. 78; Zaccheus Ellis to Mother, March 1, 1865, Zaccheus Ellis Papers, Southern Historical Collection, University of North Carolina, Chapel Hill. A copy is also at the Brunswick Town State

Historic Site, Winnabow, North Carolina. Diary entry of February 18, 1865, Calder Diary, Duke; Abstract log of *U.S.S. Shawmut*, February 18, 1865, *ORN* 12, p. 37; Hagood, *Memoirs of the War of Secession*, p. 336.

29. Official records mistakenly note Lt. Robert Bond Vause's name as Robert B. Vanse. Manarin, *North Carolina Troops*, vol. 1, p. 376. General Hagood claimed that Lieutenant Vause [Hagood recorded his name as Vance] was the only Confederate soldier killed outright in action at Fort Anderson on February 18. Hagood, *Memoirs of the War of Secession*, p. 337. Thomas H. Sutton of Company C, 40th North Carolina Regiment, recalled nineteen years after the war, that Lt. William H. Harrison of Company B, 40th North Carolina, was also killed by concussion from a Union shell at Fort Anderson. Thomas H. Sutton, "Fort Fisher: A Soldier's Account of the Defense of the Approaches to Wilmington," *Wilmington Daily Review*, October 21, 1884. Official military records, however, indicate that Lieutenant Harrison was present or accounted for through February, 1865. Manarin, *North Carolina Troops*, vol. 1, p. 386. See also: Manarin, *North Carolina Troops*, vol. 1, pp. 375-376 and 433; *Wilmington Daily Journal*, February 20, 1865; Eugene S. Martin, *Defense of Fort Anderson* (Wilmington, 1901); Hagood, *Memoirs of the War of Secession*, p. 338.

30. *New York Herald*, February 23, 1865.

31. Diary entry of February 18, 1865, Calder Diary, Duke; Hagood, *Memoirs of the War of Secession*, pp. 337-338.

32. Hagood, *Memoirs of the War of Secession*, p. 336.

33. Zaccheus Ellis to Mother, March 1, 1865, Zaccheus Ellis Papers, Southern Historical Collection; Hagood, *Memoirs of the War of Secession*, pp. 336-338; Sutton, "Defense of Wilmington," *Wilmington Daily Review*, October 21, 1884.

34. Abstract log of *U.S.S. Nyack*, February 18, 1865, *ORN* 12, p. 35; Temple to Bailey, February 21, 1865, ibid, p. 34.

35. Report of Jacob D. Cox, May 15, 1865, *OR* 47, pt. 1, pp. 960-961; Abstract from journal of Jacob D. Cox, February 18, 1865, ibid, p. 929; Hagood, *Memoirs of the War of Secession*, p. 335.

36. Hagood, *Memoirs of the War of Secession*, p. 337; Manarin, *North Carolina Troops*, vol. 1, p. 347.

37. Abstract from journal of Jacob D. Cox, February 18, 1865, *OR* 47, pt. 1, p. 929; Report of Jacob D. Cox, May 15, 1865, ibid, pp. 960-961; Cox, *March to the Sea*, p. 150; Report of Oscar W. Sterl, April 28, 1865, *OR* 47, pt. 1, p. 965; Cox to Campbell, February 18, 1865, ibid, pt. 2, p. 482; James M. Merrill and James F. Marshall, (eds.) "The 16th Kentucky and the End of the Civil War: The Letters of Henry Clay Weaver," *Filson Club History Quarterly*, p. 32 (October 1958); Thomas Speed to Parents, February 25, 1865, Speed Collection, Filson Club; Hagood, *Memoirs of the War of Secession*, p. 337; "The Capture of Wilmington," *National Tribune*, January 14, 1915; Nelson Pinney, *History of the 104th Regiment Ohio Volunteer Infantry During the War of the Rebellion* (Akron, 1886), p. 75; "Journal of Adam Weaver," *Wilmington Morning Star*, December 27, 1964.

38. Reports vary as to the number of Union casualties at Orton Pond on February 18, 1865. General Cox noted in his journal on the day of the fight that he lost one man killed and seven men wounded. Abstract from journal of Jacob D. Cox, February 18, 1865, *OR* 47, pt. 1, p. 929. Colonel Oscar W. Sterl reported that "[Lieutenant Reed's] charging party lost 1 man killed and 4 wounded." Report of Oscar W. Sterl, April 28, 1865, ibid, p. 965. These figures are subsequently corroborated by Cox in his official Carolinas Campaign report of May 15, 1865. "After a brisk skirmish of half an hour," he recorded, "a passage was effected with 1 killed and 4 wounded." Report of Jacob D. Cox, May 15, 1865, ibid, p. 961. Confederate casualties are unknown. See also Cox to Campbell, February 18, 1865, *OR* 47, pt. 2, pp. 482-483;

39. Report of Oscar W. Sterl, April 28, 1865, *OR* 47, pt. 1, p. 965; Henry Jackson and Thomas O'Donnell, *Back Home in Oneida: Hermon Clarke and His Letters* (Syracuse, 1965), p. 192; Report of Jacob D. Cox, May 15, 1865, *OR* 47, pt. 1, p. 961; Cox to Schofield, February 18, 1865, ibid, pt. 2, p. 482; Cox to Campbell, February 18, 1865, ibid, pp. 482-483; "The Capture of Wilmington," *National Tribune*, January 14, 1915.

40. William Calder to Mother, February 10, 1865, Calder Papers, Southern Historical Collection.

41. *Wilmington Daily Journal*, February 18, 1865.

42. Zaccheus Ellis to Mother, March 1, 1865, Zaccheus Ellis Papers, Southern Historical Collection; Barrett, *The Civil War in North Carolina*, p. 282; Hagood, *Memoirs of the War of Secession*, p. 337; Abstract log of *U.S.S. Yantic*, February 18-19, 1865, *ORN* 12, p. 36; Diary entry of February 18, 1865, Calder Diary, Duke.

43. Cushing Journal, National Archives. According to one Union sailor, Cushing supervised the construction of the "Quaker monitor" February 13-14. Diary entries of February 13-14, 1865, Hern Diary, Morris L. Yoder, Jr. collection, Philadelphia; *Raleigh Semi-Weekly Standard*, March 24, 1865; Temple to Bailey, February 21, 1865, *ORN* 12, p. 34; Abstract log of *U.S.S. Malvern*, February 13-16, 1865, *ORN* 12, p. 174.

44. Accounts differ as to the night Porter and Cushing deployed the phony monitor against Fort Anderson. Porter's book of wartime anecdotes published twenty years after the conflict, seemed to indicate that he used the sham monitor on the night of February 16. "The night before we attacked that place I had a mock monitor towed up and let go within two hundred yards of the enemy works." Porter, *Incidents and Anecdotes*, p. 275. That date and time was corroborated by the wartime diary of George Hern, a landsman aboard the *Sassacus*. "16th, clear and moonlight," Hern recorded, "Sent Quaker Monitor up at 11 PM." Diary entry of February 16, 1865, Hern Diary, Morris L. Yoder, Jr. collection, Philadelphia. William B. Cushing reported in his postwar journal that he cast the ironclad adrift off Fort Anderson on the night of February 18. He recorded a detailed account of the incident and noted: "We took possession [of Fort Anderson] next morning." Cushing Journal, National Archives. February 18 is supported by at least two contemporary newspaper accounts written by reporters on the scene. Elias Smith of the *New York Tribune* reported on February

19: "Admiral Porter played another of his Yankee tricks upon the enemy last night. . .His mock monitor was cautiously towed up close under the guns of the fort about 10 o'clock. . . ." *New York Tribune*, February 23, 1865. A *New York Herald* correspondent, Thomas M. Cook, also wrote on February 19 a good account of the ruse. "The affair was towed up close to the fort at ten o'clock last evening and then cast adrift. . . ." *New York Herald*, February 23, 1865. It is unlikely the fake monitor was used on both February 16 and 18. All but one account reported that she drifted past Fort Anderson and grounded on the east side of the Cape Fear River behind Confederate lines. The logbook of Admiral Porter's flagship *Malvern* suggests that Cushing employed *Old Bogey* on February 18. The entry for that date noted that "at 9:45 [p.m.] Lieutenant Cushing and picket launch No. 6 proceeded upriver on an expedition." Presumably, "expedition" meant deployment of the sham monitor. Abstract log of *U.S.S. Malvern*, February 18, 1865, *ORN* 12, p. 174.

45. *New York Tribune*, February 23, 1865; Temple to Bailey, February 21, 1865, *ORN* 12, p. 34. "The consequence was," Lieutenant Commander Cushing boasted, "that the commanding Confederate knowing that the army was closing in behind him and thinking a monitor in the river above--evacuated in haste. Confederate officers told me afterwards that this was the true reason for the retreat." Cushing Journal, National Archives. The *New York Herald* perpetuated the myth that the fake monitor caused the Confederates to evacuate Fort Anderson. The *Herald* reported that the "Admiral's bogus Monitor, doubtless, was the influential cause of the precipitate abandonment by the rebels of their strong defensive line on the river." *New York Herald*, February 23, 1865. Gideon Welles recorded in his diary that on February 22, 1865, "young Cushing came in with the intelligence of the capture of Fort Anderson. I went with him to see the President." Welles, *Diary of Gideon Welles*, vol. 2, p. 245. Admiral Porter reported that after the fake monitor floated past Fort Anderson, "the [Confederates] vamoosed as a deserter informed us, 'the damned monitor having cut them off all day.'" Richard Means Thompson and Richard Wainright, eds., *Confidential Correspondence of Gustavus Vasa Fox*, 2 volumes (New York, 1918-1919), vol. 2, p. 200.

46. William Calder to Mother, February 15, 1865, Calder Papers, Southern Historical Collection.

47. Hagood, *Memoirs of the War of Secession*, pp. 338-339.

48. Hagood, *Memoirs of the War of Secession*, p. 339; Zaccheus Ellis to Mother, March 1, 1865, Zaccheus Ellis Papers, Southern Historical Collection. See also: *New York Tribune*, February 23, 1865; Diary entry of February 18, 1865, Calder Diary, Duke.

49. The Union army disagreed as to which troops were the first to enter Fort Anderson. Evidence suggests that Maj. Frank Wilcox of the 63rd Indiana Infantry led the initial wave of troops--Col. Thomas J. Henderson's skirmishers--against the fort. In his official report Henderson asserted: "if any credit attaches for the occupation of Fort Anderson, after its evacuation, it is perhaps due to those of my command to say that the skirmishers of my brigade were among the first, if not the first, to enter the fort." Report of Thomas Henderson, April 6, 1865, *OR* 47, pt. 1, p. 970. Henderson apparently wanted to see his brigade receive due recognition for its part in the victory, a desire that may have been related to an incident that occurred the previous evening, February 18. After General Cox left on his flanking movement around Orton Pond, Schofield assigned Colonel Henderson to command the troops that remained in front of Fort Anderson. Colonel Orlando Moore protested, stating that he was entitled to the command because his commission predated Henderson's. Upon Schofield's suggestion, Henderson relinquished authority in the interest of harmony. Thompson, *History of the 112th Illinois Infantry*, pp. 303-304. See also: Walter Clark, ed., *Histories of the Several Regiments and Battalions From North Carolina in the Great War 1861-'65*, 5 volumes (Goldsboro, 1901), vol. 2, p. 762; Thurstin, *History of the 111th Ohio Infantry*, p. 116; Hagood, *Memoirs of the War of Secession*, p. 339; Report of Thomas J. Henderson, April 6, 1865, *OR* 47, pt. 1, p. 969; *New York Herald*, February 25, 1865; Issac Sherwood, *Memories of the War (Toledo, 1923)*, p. 162; Diary entry of February 19, 1865, Simon Bennage Diary, Civil War Miscellaneous, U.S. Army Military History Institute, Carlisle Barracks, Pennsylvania.

50. Manarin, *North Carolina Troops*, vol. 1, pp. 386-387.

51. Thompson, *History of the 112th Illinois Infantry*, p. 304. See also: Report of Thomas J. Henderson, April 6, 1865, *OR* 47, pt. 1, p. 970; *New York Times*, March 18, 1865; Henry J. Raymond, *The Life, Public Services, and State Papers of Abraham Lincoln* (New York, 1865), pp. 673-674; Donald, *Lincoln*, p. 588.

52. Thompson, *History of the 112th Illinois Infantry*, p. 304; *New York Herald*, February 25, 1865.

53. Extract from journal of John C. Beaumont, February 19, 1865, *ORN* 12, p. 33; *New York Tribune*, February 23 and 25, 1865; *New York Herald*, February 25, 1865; Thurstin, *History of the 111th Ohio Infantry*, p. 116; Sherwood, *Memories of the War*, p. 161.

54. Asa Beetham to Annie, February 20, 1865, Asa Beetham Letters, Library of Congress, Washington, D.C.

55. Entry of February 19, 1865, Hern Diary, Morris L. Yoder, Jr. collection, Philadelphia; Murray and Bartlett, "Letters of Stephen C. Bartlett," *NCHR*, p. 78; Porter, *Naval History of the Civil War*, p. 728; Abstract log of *U.S.S. Malvern*, February 19, 1865, *ORN* 12, p. 175; Thompson, *History of the 112th Illinois Infantry*, p. 304.

56. Solon A. Carter to Wife, February 21, 1865, Solon A. Carter Papers, U.S. Army Military History Institute, Carlisle Barracks, Pennsylvania.; Report of Joseph C. Abbott, May 10, 1865, *OR* 47, pt. 1, p. 921.

57. Cox to Campbell, February 19, 1865, *OR* 47, pt. 2, p. 494; Cox to Campbell, February 19, 1865, ibid, p. 495; Abstract from journal of Jacob D. Cox, February 19, 1865, ibid, pt. 1, p. 929; Entry of February 19, 1865, Nicholas DeGraff Journal, p. 331, *Civil War Times Illustrated* Collection, U.S. Army Military History Institute, Carlisle Barracks, Pennsylvania.

58. Cox to Campbell, February 19, 1865, *OR* 47, pt. 2, p. 495; Abstract from journal of Jacob D. Cox, February 19, 1865, ibid, pt. 1, p. 929; Report of Jacob D. Cox, May 15, 1865, ibid, p. 961; *New York Herald*, February 25, 1865; Thompson, *History of the 112th Illinois Infantry*, p. 305; Report of Thomas J. Henderson, April 6, 1865, *OR* 47, pt. 1, p. 970.

CHAPTER 4: THE AFTERMATH

1. One U.S. Navy report claimed that Fort Anderson's armament comprised three rifled 32-pounders, six smoothbore 32-pounders, and three smoothbore 24-pounders. Report of David D. Porter, February 27, 1865, *ORN* 12, p. 56. Quotes are from: Schofield to Grant, February 19, 1865, *OR* 47, pt. 2, p. 493; *New York Tribune*, February 23, 1865.

2. *New York Tribune*, February 23, 1865; *New York Herald*, February 23, 1865.

3. Anderson to Hoke, February 8, 1865, *OR* 47 pt. 2, p. 1131.

4. Fonvielle, "Campaign for Wilmington and Fort Fisher," *Blue & Gray*, pp. 60-62. Quote is from Porter Memoir, p. 892, Porter Papers, Library of Congress.

5. James Laurence Sprunt, *The Story of Orton Plantation* (Wilmington, 1958), p. 28.

6. *Wilmington Daily Journal*, March 9 and 11, 1866.

7. Sprunt, *Chronicles of the Cape Fear River*, pp. 574-575.

8. Sprunt, *Orton Plantation*, pp. 14-15.

9. *Wilmington Messenger*, August 22, 1890.

10. Waddell, *A Colonial Officer and His Times*, p. 214; James G. Burr, "A Visit to Old Brunswick and the Ruins of St. Philip's Church," *The Church Messenger*, September 28, 1880.

11. Spunt, *Chronicles of the Cape Fear River*, p. 582.

12. Martin, *Defense of Fort Anderson*.

13. Sprunt, *Chronicles of the Cape Fear River*, pp. 580-583.

14. Sprunt, *Orton Plantation*, pp. 16-17.

15. Deed, James Laurence Sprunt, ET UX, ET ALS to State of North Carolina, December 22, 1952; Deed, Thomas H. Wright, Bishop, Trustee, ET ALS to State of North Carolina, April 24, 1953, copies at Brunswick Town State Historic Site, Winnabow, North Carolina.

16. Author's interview with Susan Taylor Block, Wilmington, North Carolina, July 12, 1998; Franda Pedlow, *The Story of Brunswick Town* (Winnabow, 1996), p. 63.

17. Author's interviews with Stanley A. South of Columbia, South Carolina, April 19 and July 31, 1998.

18. *Newsletter,* Brunswick County Historical Society I, 1 (September 1961).

19. Author's interviews with James A. Bartley, Brunswick Town State Historic Site, Winnabow, North Carolina, April 9 and July 23, 1998.

MANUSCRIPTS

Brunswick Town State Historic Site, Winnabow, North Carolina
    Miscellaneous Confederate Letters
Chautauqua County Historical Society, Westfield, New York
    William B. Cushing Journal
Cape Fear Museum, Wilmington, North Carolina
    Theodore J. Wagner Diary
Sarah B. Chapman Collection, Advance, North Carolina
    Charles F. Bahnson Letters
Duke University, Perkins Library, Durham, North Carolina
    William Badham, Jr. Papers
    Catherine Jane Buie Papers
    William Calder Diary
    Charles S. Powell Papers
    Joseph J. Wescoat Diary
East Carolina University, Joyner Library, Greenville, North Carolina
    William Badham Papers
Filson Club, Louisville, Kentucky
    Thomas Speed Collection
Indiana Historical Society, W.H. Smith Memorial Library, Indianapolis, Indiana
    Saunders Richard Hornbrook Diary
Library of Congress, Manuscript Department, Washington, D. C.
    Asa Beetham Letters
    David Dixon Porter Papers
Museum of the Confederacy, Richmond, Virginia
    Miscellaneus Confederate Letters
    Katherine Mason Rowland Collection
New Hanover County Public Library
    William M. Reaves Collection
North Carolina Division of Archives and History, Raleigh
    William S. Powell Papers
    George C. Tait Papers
    Zebulon B. Vance Papers
South Carolina Historical Society, Charleston
    George Hall Moffett Papers
Allan T. Strange Collection, Wilmington, North Carolina
    John Douglas Taylor Recollection
United States Army Military History Institute, Carlisle Barracks, Pennsylvania
    Solon A. Carter Papers
    Civil War Times Illustrated Collection
United States National Archives and Records Services, Washington, D.C.
    William Barker Cushing Journal, Record Group 45
University of North Carolina, Chapel Hill, Southern Historical Collection
    Stephen C. Bartlett Papers
    Macon Bonner Papers
    William Calder Papers
    W. G. Curtis Papers
    Zaccheus Ellis Papers
    Louis Hébert Autobiography
    Eugene S. Martin Papers
    Charles S. Powell Papers
    William Henry and Araminta Guilford Tripp Papers

Joseph J. Wescoat Papers
University of North Carolina at Wilmington, Randall Library, Special Collections
 Leora McEachern and Isabel Williams Collection
University of South Carolina, Columbia, South Caroliniana Collection
 Johnson Hagood Papers
 James Izlar Diary
Morris L. Yoder, Jr. Collection, Philadelphia, Pennsylvania
 George H. Hern Diary

OFFICIAL PUBLICATIONS

Records of United States Army Continental Commands 1821-1920. Record Group 393. United States National Archives and Records Services, Washington, D.C.

Supplement to the Official Records of the Union and Confederate Armies. 100 volumes. Wilmington, North Carolina: Broadfoot Publishing Company, 1994-1999.

United States Navy Department. *Official Records of the Union and Confederate Navies in the War of the Rebellion.* 30 volumes. Washington, D. C.: Government Printing Office, 1900-1901.

United States War Department. *Atlas to Accompany the Official Records of the Union and Confederate Armies.* Washington, D. C.: Government Printing Office, 1891-1895.

—. *The War of the Rebellion, A Compilation of the Official Records of the Union and Confederate Armies.* 70 volumes in 128 parts. Washington, D.C.: Government Printing Office, 1880-1901.

NEWSPAPERS

Charleston Mercury
Frank Leslie's Illustrated Newspaper
Gleason's Pictorial Drawing Room Companion
Harper's Weekly
National Tribune
New York Herald
New York Times
New York Tribune
New York World
Philadelphia Inquirer
Raleigh (NC) Daily Confederate
Raleigh Standard
Wilmington (NC) Daily Journal
Wilmington Daily North Carolinian
Wilmington Daily Review
Wilmington Journal
Wilmington Messenger
Wilmington Morning Star
Wilmington Star News

PUBLISHED PRIMARY SOURCES
(Includes Autobiographies, Diaries, Journals, Memoirs, Reminiscences and Unit Histories)

Bentley, James R., ed. "The Civil War Memoirs of Captain Thomas Speed." *The Filson Club History Quarterly*, 44 (July, 1970).

Burr, James G. "A Visit to Old Brunswick and the Ruins of St. Philip's Church." *The Church Messenger* (September, 1880).

Clark, Walter, ed. *Histories of the Several Regiments and Battalions From North Carolina in the Great War, 1861-'65.* 5 volumes. Goldsboro, North Carolina: Nash Brothers, 1901.

Cox, Jacob Dolson. *Military Reminiscences of the Civil War.* 2 volumes. New York: Charles Scribner's Sons, 1900.

Curtis, W. G. *Reminiscences of Wilmington and Southport, 1848-1900.* Southport, North Carolina: Herald Job Office, 1900.

Gaskill, J. W. *Footprints Through Dixie.* Alliance, Ohio: Bradshaw Publishing Company, 1919.

Grant, U. S. *Personal Memoirs of U.S. Grant*. 2 volumes. New York: Charles L. Webster & Company, 1885.

Gregorie, Anne King, ed. "Diary of Captain Joseph Julius Westcoat." *South Carolina Historical Magazine*, LIX (1958).

Hagood, Johnson. *Memoirs of the War of Secession*. Columbia, South Carolina: The State Company, 1910.

Hayes, Philip C. *Journal History of the One Hundred & Third Ohio Volunteer Infantry*. Toledo, Ohio: Commercial Steam Print, 1872.

Izlar, William V. *A Sketch of the War Record of the Edisto Rifles, 1861-1865*. Columbia, South Carolina: The State Company, 1914.

Lamb, William. *Colonel Lamb's Story of Fort Fisher*. Carolina Beach, North Carolina: Blockade Runner Museum, 1966.

Martin, Eugene S. *Defense of Fort Anderson*. Wilmington, North Carolina: North Carolina Society of Colonial Dames, 1901.

Merrill, James M., ed. "The Fort Fisher and Wilmington Campaign: Letters From Rear Admiral David D. Porter." *North Carolina Historical Review*, XXXV (October, 1958).

Merrill, James M. and James F. Marshall, eds. "The 16th Kentucky and the End of the Civil War: The Letters of Henry Clay Weaver." *The Filson Club History Quarterly*, 32 (October, 1958).

Murray, Paul and Stephen Russell Bartlett, Jr., eds. "The Letters of Stephen Chaulker Bartlett Aboard the *U.S.S. Lenapee*, January to August, 1865." *North Carolina Historical Review*, XXXIII (January, 1956).

Pinney, Nelson. *History of the 104th Regiment Ohio Volunteer Infantry During the War of Rebellion*. Akron, Ohio: Werner & Lohmann, 1886.

Porter, David D. *Incidents and Anecdotes of the Civil War*. New York: D. Appleton and Company, 1886.

Rowland, Kate Mason, ed. "Letters of Major Thomas Rowland, C.S.A." *William and Mary College Quarterly Historical Magazine*, XXVI (April, 1917).

Schofield, John M. *Forty-Six Years in the Army*. New York: The Century Company, 1897.

Sherman, William Tecumseh. *Memoirs of General W. T. Sherman*. 2 volumes. New York: Literary Classics of the United States, 1990.

Sherwood, Issac R. *Memoirs of the War*. Toledo, Ohio: H.J. Chittendon Co., 1923.

Simmons, Slann L. C., ed. "Diary of Abram W. Clement, 11th South Carolina Infantry, 1865." *South Carolina Historical Magazine*, LIX (1958).

Sutton, Thomas H. "Fort Fisher: A Soldiers Account of the Defense of the Approaches to Wilmington." *Wilmington (N.C.) Daily Review* (October, 21, 1884).

Thompson, B. F. *History of the 112th Regiment of Illinois Volunteer Infantry in the Great War of the Rebellion, 1862-1865*. Toulan, Illinois: Stark County News Office, 1885.

Thompson, Richard Means and Richard Wainwright, eds. *Confidential Correspondence of Gustavus Vasa Fox*. 2 volumes. New York: Naval Historical Society, 1918-1919.

Thurstin, W. S. *History One Hundred and Eleventh Regiment Ohio Volunteer Infantry*. Toledo, Ohio: Vrooman, Anderson & Bateman, 1894.

Travis, B. F. *The Story of the Twenty-Fifth Michigan*. Kalamazoo, Michigan: Kalamazoo Publishing Company, 1897.

Waddell, Alfred Moore. *Some Memories of My Life*. Raleigh, North Carolina: Edwards & Broughton Printing Company, 1908.

Welles, Gideon. *Diary of Gideon Welles*. 3 volumes. Boston and New York: Houghton Mifflin Company, 1911.

PUBLISHED SECONDARY SOURCES

Barrett, John G. *The Civil War in North Carolina*. Chapel Hill: University of North Carolina Press, 1963.

Brunswick County Historical Society. *Newsletter*. I, 1 (September, 1961).

Cox, Jacob Dolson. *Campaigns of the Civil War: The March to the Sea, Franklin and Nashville*. New York: Charles Scribner's Sons, 1900.

Davis, William C. *The Confederate General*. 6 volumes. The National Historical Society, 1991.

DeRosset, William Lord. *Pictorial and Historical New Hanover County and Wilmington, North Carolina*. Wilmington: DeRosset, 1938.

Donald, David Herbert. *Lincoln*. New York: Simon & Schuster, 1995.

Faust, Patricia L. *Historical Times Illustrated Encyclopedia of the Civil War*. New York: Harper & Row, 1986.

Fonvielle, Chris E., Jr., "The Last Rays of Departing Hope: The Campaign for Wilmington and Fort Fisher." *Blue & Gray Magazine* (December, 1994).

—. "William Barker Cushing: Commando at the Cape Fear." *Blue & Gray Magazine* (Summer, 1997).

—. *The Wilmington Campaign: Last Rays of Departing Hope*. Campbell, California: Savas Publishing, 1997.

Lee, E. Lawrence. *The Lower Cape Fear in Colonial Days*. Chapel Hill, North Carolina: University of North Carolina Press, 1971.

Lossing, Benson J. *The Pictorial Field-Book of the Revolution*. 2 volumes. (New York: Harper & Brothers, 1860).

Manarin, Louis H. and Weymouth T. Jordan, eds. *North Carolina Troops 1861-1865: A Roster*. 14 volumes. Raleigh, North Carolina: Division of Archives and History, 1966-1998.

McDonough, James L. *Schofield: Union General in the Civil War and Reconstruction*. Tallahassee: Florida State University Press, 1972.

Pedlow, Franda D. *The Story of Brunswick Town*. Winnabow, North Carolina: Brunswick Town State Historic Site, 1996.

Porter, David D. *The Naval History of the Civil War*. New York: The Sherman Publishing Company, 1886.

Raymond, Henry J. *The Life, Public Services, and State Papers of Abraham Lincoln*. New York: Derby & Miller, 1865.

Reed, Rowena. *Combined Operations in the Civil War*. Annapolis, Maryland: Naval Institute Press, 1978.

Scott, Colonel H. L. *Military Dictionary: Comprising Technical Definitions: Information on Raising and Keeping Troops, Actual Service, Including Makeshifts and Improved Materiel; and Law, Government, Regulation, and Administration Relating to Land Forces*. New York: Greenwood Press, 1968.

Seitz, Don C. *Braxton Bragg: General of the Confederacy*. Columbia, South Carolina: The State Company, 1924.

Silverstone, Paul H. *Warships of the Civil War Navies*. Annapolis, Maryland: Naval Institute Press, 1989.

South, Stanley A. "A Nice Little Fight at Fort Anderson." Unpublished manuscript, Brunswick Town State Historic Site, Winnabow, North Carolina.

Sprunt, James. *Chronicles of the Cape Fear River 1660-1916*. Raleigh, North Carolina: Edwards & Broughton Printing Co., 1916.

—. *Tales and Traditions of the Lower Cape Fear, 1661-1896*. Wilmington, North Carolina: LeGwin Brothers, 1896.

Sprunt, James Laurence. *The Story of Orton Plantation*. Wilmington, 1958.

Still, William N., Jr., "Porter Is the Best Man." *Civil War Times Illustrated*, XVI (May, 1977).

Sumner, Merlin E., ed. *The Diary of Cyrus B. Comstock*. Dayton, Ohio: Morningside Bookshop, 1987.

Waddell, Alfred Moore. *A Colonial Officer and His Times*. Raleigh, North Carolina: Edwards & Broughton, 1890.

Warner, Ezra J. *Generals In Blue*. Baton Rouge: Louisiana State University Press, 1964.

—. *Generals In Gray*. Baton Rouge: Louisiana State University Press, 1959.

Watson, Alan D. *Wilmington: Port of North Carolina*. Columbia, South Carolina: University of South Carolina Press, 1992.

Welcher, Frank J., *The Union Army, 1861-1865 Organization and Operations, Volume 1, The Eastern Theater*. Bloomington and Indianapolis: Indiana University Press, 1989.

Wise, Stephen R. *Lifeline of the Confederacy: Blockade Running During the Civil War*. Columbia: University of South Carolina Press, 1988.

INTERVIEWS

James A. Bartley
Susan Taylor Block
Stanley A. South

Index